Mathias Elsässer

Intelligent Data-Driven Marketing: When Physicists Start Thinking about Marketing

From Mad-Man to Math-Man Marketing

Mathias Elsässer

INTELLIGENT DATA-DRIVEN MARKETING: WHEN PHYSICISTS START THINKING ABOUT MARKETING

From Mad-Man to Math-Man Marketing

Bibliografische Information der Deutschen Nationalbibliothek

Die Deutsche Nationalbibliothek verzeichnet diese Publikation in der Deutschen Nationalbibliografie; detaillierte bibliografische Daten sind im Internet über http://dnb.d-nb.de abrufbar.

Bibliographic information published by the Deutsche Nationalbibliothek

Die Deutsche Nationalbibliothek lists this publication in the Deutsche Nationalbibliografie; detailed bibliographic data are available in the Internet at http://dnb.d-nb.de.

ISBN-13: 978-3-8382-1651-5
© *ibidem*-Verlag, Stuttgart 2022
Alle Rechte vorbehalten

Das Werk einschließlich aller seiner Teile ist urheberrechtlich geschützt. Jede Verwertung außerhalb der engen Grenzen des Urheberrechtsgesetzes ist ohne Zustimmung des Verlages unzulässig und strafbar. Dies gilt insbesondere für Vervielfältigungen, Übersetzungen, Mikroverfilmungen und elektronische Speicherformen sowie die Einspeicherung und Verarbeitung in elektronischen Systemen.

All rights reserved. No part of this publication may be reproduced, stored in or introduced into a retrieval system, or transmitted, in any form, or by any means (electronic, mechanical, photocopying, recording or otherwise) without the prior written permission of the publisher. Any person who does any unauthorized act in relation to this publication may be liable to criminal prosecution and civil claims for damages.

Printed in the EU

"Everything should be made as simple as possible, but not simpler.
If you can't explain it simply, you don't understand it well enough."

Albert Einstein

Contents

Introduction — #intelligentmarketing 11
Applying physics to marketing 12
Applying business engineering to marketing 14

The imaginary marketing lab, playing with data and thoughts 19
Gedankenexperiment 1.0 20
    The Marketing Universe — our inertial system of reference 20
    Starting with Audiences and Campaigns 23
    Plan the activations via different impressions 23
    Gaining a return on marketing invest 24
    Be more precise — take advantage of segmentation 24
    Close the loop — the advantage of data analysts 24
    From measures to KPIs 26
Data-Driven Marketing: Measures, KPIs, and Dimensions 26
    Share of 27
    Marketing Pressure 27
    Cost per 28
    Conversion rate 28
    Trends 29
    Aggregated KPIs of unique 30
Audience centric KPI systems 31
    Integrated Reach — a bit of both 34
Smart KPI — Reporting, Dashboarding and Data Science 35
    Pillar 1: Standard Reporting 35
    Pillar 2: Explorative Data Analytics 36
    Pillar 3: Data Science 36
Gedankenexperiment 2.0 37
    A house is not enough — strategic marketing planning 39
    Different Balls — creative management & optimization 42
    Smaller Segments — hyper-accurate targeting and look-a-likes 46
    Multiple Players — paid, owned, earned 52
    Throwing tactics — the media mix and attribution models 56
    Multiple actions — goals, funnels and customer journeys 60
    Mat Robo — trigger-based campaign automation 65
    My bag is full — frequency caps and campaign maintenance 67
    The Perpetuum mobile — sharing, communities, and influencing 72
    Summary — Gedankenexperiment 2.0 76

Using more physics on marketing 79
Fluid dynamics — "reaching the perfect flow" 80
Harmonic oscillation — "everything is in motion" 82
The law of thermodynamics — "flow of change" 85
Solid State Physics — "building out complex systems" 88
Einstein's Theory of Relativity — "There is one last thing" 91

The ma.tomics — Intelligent Data-Driven Marketing Framework 97
GW1 From counting actions to guiding audiences 98
GW2 Real-time and zero latency 99
GW3 Closed-Loop — Harmonic Oscillation 100
GW4 Mastering the Tech-Stack-Orchestration 100
GW5 Run Agile — Start Fast and Fail Fast 101
GW6 Enable the organization 103
M1 THE MARKETING UNIVERSE 105
    M1.1 Get Your Fundamentals Right: Strategy, Process, and Systems 105
    M1.2 Understand and Engage with your Customer: Audience and Content Management 106
    M1.3 Take the right budget choices: Strategic Investment Management 108
M2 MARKETING TAXONOMY 110
    M2.1 Align on a corporate taxonomy: Hidden Data Asset 110
    M2.2 Embrace Change: Master Data Governance "Customer, Campaigns, Content, Asset, Price & Finance" 111
M3 STRATEGIC PORTFOLIO & PROGRAM MANAGEMENT 113
    M3.1 Program, Audience, Content, and Time Management 113
    M3.2 Marketing Budget Management 114
    M3.3 Plan Alignment, Innovation, and Collaboration 116
M4 CREATIVE MANAGEMENT 118
    M4.1 Creative Ideation — Design Thinking 119
    M4.2 Creative Development and Delivery 120
    M4.3 Creative Optimization 122
M5 AGILE CAMPAIGNS MANAGEMENT 124
    M5.1 Be Fast and Flexible: Campaign Preparation 124
    M5.2 Run Fast, Fail Fast: Campaign Execution 126
    M5.3 Manage Trigger-Based Campaigns: Campaign Automation 128

M6 PROFILING — KNOWN & UNKNOWN AUDIENCES 130
- M6.1 The golden record of your customers 130
- M6.2 The "Known-Unknown" Asset of Audience Data 132
- M6.3 Fundamental base work — Content Tagging 133
- M6.4 Consent Management — Customer Buy-In 134
- M6.5 Data Protection — Legal and Legitimate 136

M7 HYPER ACCURATE TARGETING and LOOK-A-LIKE 139
- M7.1 Plan & Design — Strategic Audiences 139
- M7.2 Build & Activate — Tactical Segments 141
- M7.3 Reach is King — Accurate Targets and Higher Reach 143

M8 INNOVATIVE & OPTIMIZED PEO ACTIVATION MIX 145
- M8.1 Paid (Media) Activations 145
- M8.2 Earned (Media) Attention 147
- M8.3 Owned Touchpoint orchestration 148
- M8.4 Social and Voice — two special capabilities 151
- M8.5 Planning Pricing & Trade Promotions 152
- M8.6 Media Mix Planning and Optimization 154

M9 GET VIRAL — SHARING ECONOMY OF SCALES 156
- M9.1 Tweets, Likes, and Shares 156
- M9.2 AI Image Processing and Sentiment Analysis 158

M10 THE MOST EFFECTIVE FLOW OF ACTIONS 160
- M10.1 Multi-Touch Attribution Models 160
- M10.2 Large Scale A/B testing & 1:1 journeys 162
- M10.3 Machine Learning — AI-Driven Optimizations 163
- M10.4 Goal and Funnel management 165
- M10.5 The Law of Action and Reaction — High Performing Machines 167

M11 CUSTOMER INTIMACY — DEMAND WINDOWS AND PRICING 169
- M11.1 Find the Right Moment in Time — Demand Windows 169
- M11.2 Find the best context — Demand Windows 170
- M11.3 Find the Best Price — Data-Driven Pricing Windows 172

M12 CROSS DEVICE AND PLATFORMS 174
- M12.1 Cross-Device Identification — ID Strategies 174
- M12.2 Cross-Platform Profiles 176

M13 MEASURE REACH, SUCCESS & AWARENESS 179
- M13.1 Integrated Reach 180
- M13.2 Brand Awareness 181
- M13.3 eCom — Direct to customer models 182
- M13.4 Offline — Retail — Brick and Mortar Models 184
- M13.5 General — Market Intelligence and Surveys 186

M14 CONNECT SALES 188
    M14.1 Marketing Mix Modelling — Incremental Sales Uplifts 188
    M14.2 Trade Promotion Effects and Pricing 190

M15 STAY LEAN AND SHARE — SMART KPIs 192
    M15.1 Stay Lean: Measures, KPIs, and Dimensions 192
    M15.2 Share Your Data Assets: The New Imperative 194

M16 EXPLORATIVE REPORTING AND DATA SCIENCE 196
    M16.1 Get the Basics: Standard Reporting 196
    M16.2 Explorative Insights 198
    M16.3 Working Data Science 199

M17 PREDICT THE FUTURE 201
    M17.1 Programmatic Program and Campaign Planning 201
    M17.2 Next Best Action 202
    M17.3 Text, Image, and Voice Recognition 204

M18 THERE IS ONE LAST THING — CREATIVITY 205
    M18.1 Engage With Your Audience — Creativity is King 205
    M18.2 Create Emotions — Storytelling and Purposeful Marketing 207

From Mad-Men to Math-Men Marketing 209

Works Cited 219

Introduction — #intelligentmarketing

It's been a while since I embarked on this journey to write this book on marketing. Many people were directing the same question over and over again to me: why are you pursuing this? This was followed by the statement, "You are a physicist and not a marketeer." So, why should someone read this book?

For me, the answer is crystal clear; it's also the reason I started this project, which is based on sessions I've hosted in the past few years as a business consultant for data-driven marketing. It's the feedback I've received — this was the reason! Over the years, I had a lot of positive feedback, and they all said similar things, such as: "Thank you, Mathias, for this fresh view on the marketing universe and the fundamental work on reducing the complexity to the pure and really necessary facts without blowing this all up with endless digital bullshit bingo."

For this reason alone, I hope this book will help you gain fresh insight on marketing and the core principles that are still valid in this fast-moving, digital, and data-driven marketing world. This book follows my thoughts on how to reduce complexity to define the inner core of data-driven marketing. Later, it adds more advice and dimensions step-by-step, to express the real world in a smart framework.

Keep in mind while you're reading each chapter, that people in a static position, fast-moving watches passing them run slower. This is Einstein's relativity theory! We should build "run fast fail fast" data-driven marketing machines, allowing us to harvest a marketing universe in lightspeed and real-time.

So please, follow me on this journey of applying physics to marketing, and I hope that you enjoy it.

Mathias Elsässer
January, 2021

Applying physics to marketing

Let me take you back to the time I was studying physics at KIT (Karlsruhe Institute of Technology). It was a little while ago now, but I still vividly recall this wonderful, air-conditioned lab that was completely dark. It was on the upper floors of the "Physics-Skyscraper," and was the only way to escape this unnatural "tropical" summers in the lower valley of river Rhine city of Karlsruhe. There was a rumor, that long ago, a former King of Germany sent his soldiers to fight for new territories in Africa to Karlsruhe since rain with temperatures above 23 °C is quite common there.

Long story short, it's easy to imagine that I've spent a lot of my time sitting in this wonderful, cool laboratory that was void of sunshine at the end of my physics study. To be honest, the total darkness was also a good way to escape my professor's ongoing "let's have a Gedankenexperiment" lesson. He was young, had just relocated from MIT, and he loved to play with his scholars. I'm not sure whether he did those lessons to challenge us, encouraging us to learn, or it was so that he could feel far more powerful and smarter than us.

My diploma thesis was planned in two phases: the first one included setting up the laboratory and the experiment, so I could measure the unpredicted switch-off-on effects of semiconductor micro-lasers. I won't go too in-depth on the subject matter since this is a book about marketing after all, but the effect I wanted to achieve (that I'd spent nearly a year of my life on) was the tiny lasers completely switching off in case you pump them up with a push of extra energy. The most logical solution — and the behavior that is expected — is to increase the illumination, measured easily as a more powerful output laser beam. With the huge laser pumped up through dozens of mirrors, we produced a tiny microlaser which finally ended up in an infrared camera to measure the output. It took me two whole months to set this up and calibrated. I had to do this before I could measure the first laser beams — including the picosecond short switch-off-on effect.

Once this was done, I started the second phase. The goal was to replicate the curves I'd measured exactly, and this was using the Maxwell equations. It was the advent of PCs and the institute I was working for had ten of the 80286 Hewlett Packard PCs — what unbelievable computing power back in the day! We decided to veer away from the standard to buy computer time on a big Grey mainframe for all the calculations. We started what we would call hyper parallel processing nowadays. Every evening, I occupied all ten PCs and started a joined calculation of my Maxwell equation simulation C++ program. The results were very impressive, and we found an answer to the switch-off-on effect. Are you curious? Here is the full solution (M. Elsässer, 1997): "Subpicosecond switch-off and switch-on of a semiconductor laser due to transient hot carrier effects."

But I'm sure you are more curious about the reason why this marketing book begins with a historic account about a lab and the laser experiments that were conducted. Well, that's an easy thing to answer. When I looked back (years later, might I add), it was these 12 months that included the most important information you need to know when you're contemplating data-driven marketing.

Let's start with the most important lesson we can take out of this case:

> **It is possible to measure the real world and to simulate it via predictive IT models**

The word 'measure' in this context means focusing on the core measures and then start thinking about the further calculations (the equations) and rules behind what we call today KPIs and predictive models. The interesting information to glean from the short story above is that you can measure the pump-up power, the power of the laser output, the frequency of the laser wave, the outside temperatures (which was as mentioned this lovely cool and stable 18 °C in our case), and the one inside the tiny microlaser. All of these are certainly time-dependent and were measured on a femtosecond timeline — that's it. Some people expected a complex set of hundreds of attributes that needs to be measured — well they were wrong, to say the least. We are talking about four to five time-dependent core measures and four Maxwell formulas, that's all there is to it. This allows us to simulate an intricate physical experiment, and to predict the picosecond switch-off-on effect of semiconductor micro-lasers, due to transient hot carrier effects.

The other information that you would learn from the story is that:

> **A Gedankenexperiment could help postulate hypotheses to understand the rules defining the real world.**

In most cases, there will be an equation to simulate the real world in various ways, which we now call "predictive models". An example of the equation would be the Maxwell Equations in my thesis case. In terms of marketing (what you're here for!) I will explain the model in the following next chapters.

Everyone should keep in mind that the first initial gut feeling and thoughts about the expected behavior of a complex system, more often than not, aren't true. It takes time to understand the hidden rules in the system you focus on. The easiest way to get behind the miracles of complex systems is to reduce the complexity as much as you can. Reduce it to the fundamental core and, step by step, add in the isolated facts and dimensions later on so you can finally reach a theoretical copy of the real world.

Another thing for you to know is that the mythos of super-computer predicting in real-time isn't true. In today's world of artificial intelligence and machine learning, computer power is always limited. Independent from the newest innovation, the latest predictive models will consume the maximum available power for the moment to get at least a really short view of the future.

> Finally, painful but true, there is always somebody out with a more powerful brain than you, which forces us to think twice to understand his thoughts and theories.

Applying business engineering to marketing

In the meantime, just six years after leaving KIT, I started a new job as a Project Manager in the software industry. To me, it was obvious that physics and some business experience wasn't nearly enough to have a great understanding of the market and business models of big enterprises. I thought for a while and came up with a new plan. I was going to gain more experience and develop the knowledge and skills I already had by learning with a hands-on in international business management. I did some research and found that an executive MBA looked like the perfect fit for me. It would broaden my existing knowledge within physics, software development, and complex business processes. This aside, let's bring the focus back on fundamental learning which will be applied to marketing in the following chapters.

The famous University of St. Gallen teaches us that enterprises can't be changed in the classical way of "this is my new To-Be world, let's move on there." Instead, to run a successful transformation you have to follow the way of business engineering (Österle & Winter, 2003) to change your business so that it's running parallel to your daily work.

It is only this that guarantees your cash flow will remain 'alive' as well as earn the money for that necessary change. In comparison, this is like switching the engine of the plane while it's up in the air and traveling over the ocean. And of course, once you've started, there's no going back!

Business engineering is analyzing and shaping the three worlds of 'As-Is,' 'To-Be', and the realistic transformation roadmap. This is completed using different levels of strategy, processes, organization, and platforms, as well as underlying data models. All of these are flanked by the soft disciplines of agility, change management, and the injection of new competencies to your existing organization.

Let's have a look at the dance of change (Senge, 1999) in modern marketing departments. Historically, most modern marketing departments are built up by creative people in sneakers and raw denim blue jeans, and they're dealing with campaigns, creatives, impressions, clicks, and GRPs. All of this is done through a marketing supply chain consisting of headquarters' marketing personnel, plus their teams, local country responsibilities, and a final regional execution via agency networks on various media channels. Apart from the section of the organization focusing on paid advertising campaigns, it's normal to see other departments involved with communities, events, sponsoring, trade promotions, retail, and sales support. Make sure you don't forget the holy communication teams dealing with press releases and partner networks; often, they're responsible for the enterprise-owned mobile apps, webpages, bots, and newsletters.

But market-led strategic change (Piercy, 2001) takes care about the view and emotions of your customer (B2B) or consumer (B2C) and this is why isolated departments that work on islands of proprietary processes, platforms and data-models no longer work, and ultimately, in the long run, will fail.

Enterprises that can engineer and transform their different departments in a closed-loop engine to plan, prepare, execute and control all paid, owned, and earned marketing activities and touch-points will gain a competitive advantage (Porter, 1985). This type of system is too hard for your competitors to copy; it will also aid you in staying ahead of your current competitors by designing perfect customer experiences and emotions. As a result, you direct your focus away from optimizing the single sale, and instead re-direct it into putting the customers at the forefront of your strategy and daily operations. It is an outside-in approach that burns down the classic setup of different departments and their regional country sub-teams, including the historic distinct processes of advertising, sales, and customer care.

The topic of transforming your marketing isn't a "Should I do it or not?" question — yes, you should do it, no matter what. The only question a modern CMO has to ask himself is when and how does he want to enter the new world of intelligent data-driven marketing. It's a given that in most cases, this journey will be long and arduous. If we look at the theories of disruptive innovations from Clayton Christensen (Christensen, 1997) these rules can easily be applied to the complex setup of big brands and their marketing departments. Instead of getting leaner and removing the historic ballast, high sophisticated frameworks of KPIs, and data science, there are new marketing clouds and a vast range of media channels like bots and programmatic activations, creative optimizations, and predictive models that get introduced. This all ends up in a ridiculously over-engineered setup. Smaller, leaner startup businesses, who are based on clear and easy processes, will enter the market and will do better than the giant corporations. This is because of their quick, agile ways of attracting their customers. Christensen calls this "imprisoned."

After 23 years of helping dozens of global clients optimize the way they use marketing, it's the perfect time for me to apply the knowledge I've gained and sketch out a general 'best practice' for closed-loop campaign management and intelligent data-driven marketing.

In various workshops, I've faced the challenge of explaining this to CMOs as well as implementing this in their departments and teams — a more challenging feat, I must admit. This is why I've reduced how difficult and complex marketing can come across as and teach only the core elements. This helps business owners and their teams understand it better, as this way removes the jargon and doesn't confuse them. Months ago, I began to design this holistic marketing universe and break it down into tiny elements, which I've called ma.tomics. For me, they are the smallest elements of the marketing world. Each of them contains individual bits of information about data-driven marketing, and this can all be 'stitched' (or put together) to gain a better understanding of the complicated subject.

The first part of this book will explain what I've mentioned above more in-depth and applies physics to marketing with one fundamental Gedankenexperiment. This is to reduce the complexity we see today in all marketing departments. In the second step, we will see a model 2.0 that will help to bring the dimensions and constraints modern CMOs have to deal with back.

I will use these initial thoughts about marketing later on in this book, using physics, disciplines, and frameworks to explain marketing from a physicist who has more than 20 years of experience in marketing.

The second part of the book explains the ma.tomics frameworks which give you, the reader, a clear list of interdependent atoms to be implemented within your transformation program to change your company to a fully data-driven organization.

The book will end with the last part how to transform your current way of doing marketing. From Mad-Men towards a Math-Men marketing operating model.

The imaginary marketing lab, playing with data and thoughts

Some readers may be familiar with the way famous Albert Einstein explained his general theory of relativity — some may not, so I'll explain to anyway. As this topic and framework is far too complex for an easy experiment in a laboratory, he started playing around with thoughts in a Gedankenexperiment about dark elevators. This is quite common in the world of natural science; Schrödinger's cat gained some publicity — even outside the world of physics.

One of the most popular stories is the final exam of Danish first Nobel Prize winner Nils Bohr (Wikipedia, 2017). As a young physics student at the University of Copenhagen, Nils was once faced with the following question in one of his exams: "Describe how to determine the height of a skyscraper using a barometer."

He replied, "Tie a long piece of string to the barometer, lower it from the roof of the skyscraper to the ground. The length of the string plus the length of the barometer will equal the height of the building."

This answer angered the examiner, who then decided that Nils had failed immediately. However, the student appealed because the answer was indisputably correct, and the university appointed an independent arbiter to decide. The arbiter decided that the answer was indeed correct, but that it didn't display any noticeable knowledge of physics. To resolve the problem, the decision was made to allow the student six minutes over the phone to explain his answer. For the first five minutes, the student sat in silence, his forehead creased in thought. When the arbiter pointed out that time was running out, the student replied that he had several relevant answers but couldn't decide which one to use. He then began to explain:

"Firstly, you could take a barometer up to the roof of the skyscraper, drop it over the edge, and measure the time it takes to reach the ground, but that would result in damaging the barometer.

"If the sun is shining, you could measure the height of the barometer, then set it on an edge and measure the length of its shadow. Then, you measure the length of the skyscraper's shadow, and thereafter, it's a simple matter of proportional arithmetic.

"If you wanted to be highly scientific, you could tie a short piece of string to the barometer and swing it as a pendulum, first at ground level, then on the roof of the skyscraper. The height of the building can be calculated from the difference in the pendulum's period.

"If the skyscraper has an outside emergency staircase, it would be easy to walk up to it and mark off the height in barometer lengths.

"If you wanted to be boring and orthodox, of course, you could use the barometer to measure the air pressure on the roof of the skyscraper and the ground and convert the difference into a height of air.

"But since we are continually being urged to seek new ways of doing things, the best way would be to knock on the janitor's door and say, 'If you would like a nice new barometer, I will give you this one if you tell me the height of this building.'"

In his youth, Nils played as a goalkeeper in soccer. On one occasion, his team was playing against a German side, with most of the action taking place in the German half of the field. Suddenly, the German team counterattacked, and a spectator had to shout to warn Nils about the opposition coming towards him, who was using the goalpost to write down a mathematical problem.

Right, enough of the stories and physics: it's time to enter into the wonderful world of marketing by taking a look at our virtual lab, and setting up an 'experiment' to see how marketing works and how it can be measured.

Gedankenexperiment 1.0

The Marketing Universe — our inertial system of reference

So, we are finally beginning our marketing and physics journey; we will start by stripping down the marketing universe to its basic core.

One of the first things we need to consider is that even with the advent of intelligent and predictive models, data-driven platforms, etc. the underlying process hasn't changed in any fundamental way over the last few centuries!

In the early days of mad-men marketing, the way they ran their marketing campaign by compiling and starting a campaign with a huge bout of creativity and innovation, then collect the impressions (how many people saw the advertisement once). Then, they just hoped that the result was an increase in sales, which would mean the campaign was a success. All the gained insights could be easily compiled on one sheet of paper for each campaign. Intuition and 'gut feeling' were the predominant feelings they wanted to instill into potential customers through their most successful channels.

Mad-Men Marketing

#budget

#creativity

#sales

Data-Driven Marketing

#budget
#datatables

#creativity

#sales #conversion

Math-Men Marketing

#audiences

#budget
#datacubes

#creativity

#sales #conversion
#experience

Over the last 20 years, with the advent of the digital marketing space, it has become more common to go beyond impressions, GRPs (gross rating points — this equals how many times you reach someone in a pre-defined group) and market-shares. The new trend was to add more additional measures to the ecosystem. The most prominent in trend is the "click" and "like" that has been linked to multi-layered marketing and sales funnel. For decades, the conversion rate was the central KPI. For the first time, e-Com business models could attribute marketing activations to direct user actions. The underlying process didn't change, you still had to collect data to input them in a nice spreadsheet and analyze the figures to find the most promising activation channels and creative assets. The main difference, however, was the replacement of the mad men's 'gut feelings' by hard facts managed by math-men.

With the advent of audience-driven marketing platforms, we entered the world of intelligent data-driven marketing. This means we steered away from simply counting impressions and clicks/likes and these measures with events caused by individuals. Modern marketing clouds enable you to follow your prospects, customers, or consumers through how they navigate within the digital and partly non-digital ecosystem. This collection of audience-based data allows us to make the customer journeys a priority within our marketing and sales funnel, and to segment our target groups individually. Quite often, activations are automatically based on trigger events to push your target audience to the next level in their customer journey. The structure and the amount of used data have changed while counting the impressions of a campaign; they end up in a single aggregated number. Counting the single event of getting an impression easily can break through the barrier of millions of data points per campaign.

If the process hasn't changed, we can imagine that this will in the future. A stable process or system of reference is perfect for every physicist; it allows them to strip down the complexity to the core and start thinking about the 'what-if' scenarios in a theoretical world. Welcome to the world of Gedankenexperiments.

The original intention of my Marketing Gedankenexperiment was to explain to some of my younger team colleagues about the underlying principles of marketing and the KPIs frequently used in this domain. These KPIs include impressions, GRPs, clicks, likes, and conversions. I realized that it also helped me to reduce the jungle of measures, KPIs, and mystic formulas, and provides a clear and easy model to explain the fundamental way marketing works.

Starting with Audiences and Campaigns

It all starts with the selection of a group of people we can reach with any possible interaction we can think of. Let's call this our *universe* and it represents the number of people in our virtual laboratory.

We may repeat our experiment or have multiple 'houses' in parallel, so we should give this closed space a name — let's go for the *campaign*. This means a campaign defines a virtual space (like a house, for example) in a certain amount of time. The door of this house is open and everybody interested within our defined marketing universe can see inside, and access it without issues. To sum this up, we have a huge group called the universe, which is our starting point and a sub-set of people within our closed space (the campaign house) that we defined. This strategic *audience* of interested people is now the starting point of our next steps.

Plan the activations via different impressions

If we want to interact with our audience, we need to have a way to reach them first. In my virtual lab, a bunch of balls looks like a good way to do this. This means before starting anything, we need to purchase a box of balls that we want to throw out to our audience. At first, there are costs involved for sure, but you can't get balls for free. This is only for the moment though, as it will certainly change later on as we get further into our experiments.

For the next steps, it's all about setting a goal. Now, there are two options when it comes down to this. The first is to 'hit' as many individual people as possible, whether the ball makes contact with their head, shoulder, front/back, or legs. We are solely interested in *reaching* them and getting their attention. The second option is to throw the ball in a way so the people can catch the balls. It gives them the motivation to perform the predefined *action* of "catching a ball." Regardless of the goal that's chosen, in both cases, we need to measure how many people we reached. In the second case, we also need to count the amount of successfully caught balls.

Gaining a return on marketing invest

So far, this has cost us a lot of money and we haven't seen any cash flowing back into our pockets. Therefore, an innovative solution to this would be to begin selling baskets — it might sound bizarre but stay with me here. Since people are attempting to catch the balls, they will need a basket to put their balls in. So, start selling them, say in the corner of the house, then place a short disclaimer on each ball on where they can buy baskets — this is a clear *call to action*. As we have set a price for each basket, we get some money flowing back into our pockets. This is a *return on our investment* from our costly balls, which is caused by the customers trying to catch a ball and finally deciding that they should get a basket, and follow the disclaimer (the message on the ball) Let's find a better name, something related to marketing, for our disclaimer — what about *creative (or something a bit more general) branded content?*

Be more precise — take advantage of segmentation

As we proceed with our campaign by throwing the balls, it may become clearer that there's a difference between the success rate of caught balls with people of different height. Taller people are more likely to be hit in comparison to those who aren't taller 1.70 m. So, it makes sense to build two targets: the "tall" and "medium-sized" people in the house. Let's name them *"tall" and "medium" segments*.

The same principles can be applied if our goal is to reach as many people as possible by throwing the ball. If we cut the floor of our main audience into two sections — with the first half directly in front of us and the second half towards the back of the room. Based on this "front" and "back" segmentation, we can tailor our throwing technique. They would be soft throws in the front and straight long-distance strikes for the second segment further away from us.

Close the loop — the advantage of data analysts

To stay on top of the game and avoiding losing insights, we add a second player to the game who doesn't throw any balls. Instead, they are responsible for counting the balls, money, and people we reached — I'd like to call him a real data analyst. Each number in the described game above is carefully collected by him. On a whiteboard, the analyst will update the numbers of his findings every minute (latency).

On the whiteboard, there will be a table; the rows are used for the fundamental classifications that I like to call *dimensions*, and the second part of columns is the ongoing updated part of the *measures* we'd like to count in our lab.

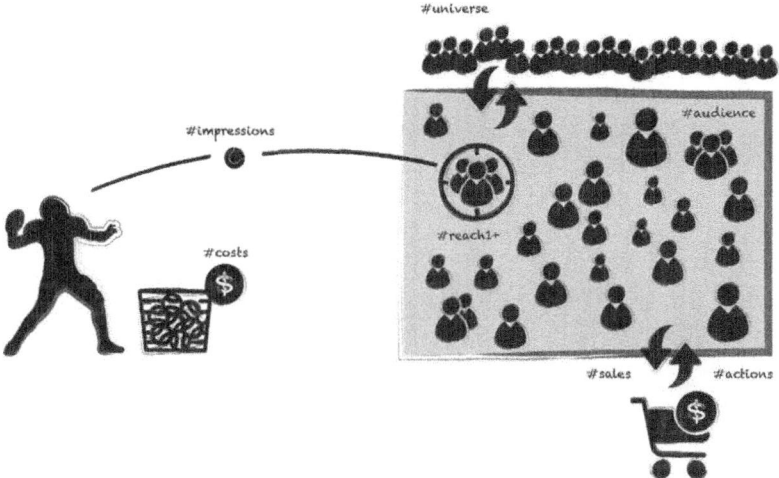

Dimensions:

- The name of our house → *campaign*
- The people attracted by our house → *audience*
- The way we clustered them → *segments*
- The fact that this number is a plan or the real thing → *plan/actual*

Measures:

- The possible number of people who can enter the house → *universe*
- The size of each segment → *segment sizes*
- How many balls we have in our basket and how much we paid for them → *(planned) impressions and costs*
- How many we have thrown so far and the correlated cost of the balls → *(actual) impressions and costs*
- How many times we hit someone → *gross reach*
- How many people we hit → *net reach*
- How many times someone has caught a ball → *conversions/actions*
- How many baskets we sold → *sales amount*

Our data analyst is a really smart guy! He always takes a photo of the board just before he updates the numbers at the end of each minute. The photo is then printed out and stuck on the wall behind the whiteboard in a linear sequence. At the end of the experiment, it's obvious that most of the measures have a strong time dependency on each other. While the universe looks stable, the amount of gross, net reach, etc. is different on each picture in our time-sequence.

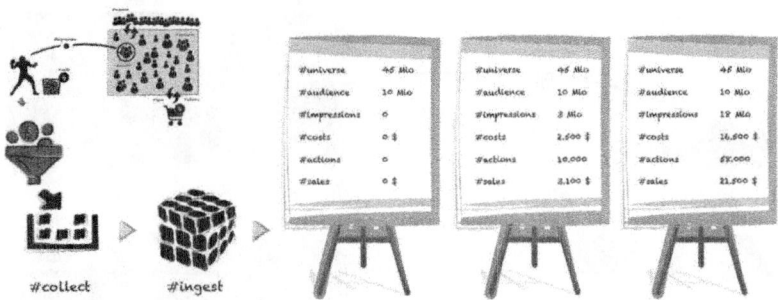

Well, that's it as we can't measure much more in our lab. I'm sure you have a few more things in mind but for the sake of easiness and clarity, I'd like to leave them here and open a second, more advanced, Gedankenexperiment 2.0 later in this book.

To summarize this experience, there are only two hand-full of measures and a very limited set of dimensions to describe a stable inertial system of reference for marketing. It's important to mention in this summary that it isn't possible to measure things like shares and the cost per ball because it's all part of an overarching framework on top of our core experiment that uses the measures to go beyond pure reporting of the things we "see."

From measures to KPIs

Therefore, the next step is the need to add additional brainwork into the game and combine the measures we have to, more powerful *KPIs*.

Data-Driven Marketing: Measures, KPIs, and Dimensions

If you have followed the Gedankenexperiment thoroughly, then you'll see it's clear that we have three distinct types of things we can use on our whiteboard to stay on top of what happens in the lab.

First up are the things we can measure and the second is our classification — the dimensions. They tell us when and where we have measured these values. Finally, the real asset is the key performance indexes (KPIs) we're now able to calculate out of the measures.

Curious? Good! Now, let's focus on the calculation and do some of the brain work I've mentioned at the end of the previous chapter.

Share of ...

I'd like to start with some basics — often it's much easier to compare shares of the total universe and frequencies instead of dealing with the actual number of people we reached (our net reach#) and the number of times we are hitting someone with our balls (gross reach#). The portion of the whole group allows us to deal with scales per hundred and, for this reason, comparison becomes much easier. The trade-off is that often, the reference group for the calculation isn't obvious and may allow room for interpretations. So, should we report the percentage of the universe, the audience group of people attracted to our house, or the final tactical segment of tall people? Most of the time it's the first one, but make sure you cross-check whenever you start dealing with percentage values.

In 20 years of consulting, I've seen dozens of marketing professionals comparing some shares without knowing the initial total this is calculated on. So, let me just explain here: "percent = per one hundred", which means the number of people has been normalized to a total group of a hundred. Thus, without knowing the total group, each percentage value is worthless!

Since we now have the same value in the form of a percentage value and the absolute value, we need to find a way to distinguish them, which is why I've added a # for absolute numbers and a % for the percentages of a defined total reference.

Besides the shares, we can also bring two measures into a relationship. In most cases, we will end-up in some kind of frequency.
With the measures universe#, net, and gross reach# we can calculate:

$$net\ reach\ \% = \frac{net\ reach\ \#}{universe\ \#} \times 100\% \qquad frequency = \frac{gross\ reach\ \#}{net\ reach\ \#}$$

Marketing Pressure

If we don't care about the fact that one person may catch more than one ball or if more people catch just one ball, we can then define another KPI that express some kind of marketing pressure we put on our universe. Again, we're going to run the challenge to first decide which universe is the correct one, similarly to our % calculation above.

This new KPI helps us to compare several iterations of our campaign and we've called it *"gross rating points (GRP)."* It's calculated by the following metric:

$$GRP = net\ reach\ \% \times frequency$$

Cost per ...

Now, let us factor in the cost and combine this with the number of balls (impressions) we bought, as well as the success we've seen in the form of sold baskets. To deal with lower numbers (normally for huge amounts of impressions per thousand (per mille) is used), this eliminates three digits of zero at the end of the impressions.

We will name the two new KPIs cost per mille (CPM) and cost per action (CPA). For CPA, we should always add the dimension of the action we are referring to.

$$CPM = \frac{costs}{\left(gross\ reach\ \#/1000\right)} \qquad CPA = \frac{costs}{amount\ of\ actions\ \#}$$

Conversion rate

Anyhow, actions are a much broader topic than you think, and they are part of further calculations. Besides the new KPIs for defining the reach, frequencies, and marketing pressure in form of GRPs, it's recommended that you relate this with the expected or actual outcome. In our game, this means considering the number of balls that have been thrown, and relate this to the ones that are caught, and the baskets that are bought.

By doing this, we have a KPI that gives us a number for the conversion of dedicated actions. In the digital advertising world, every action starts with a click; often, this is called *"click-through rate (CTR)."* For now, I'd like to name it the *"conversion rate."*

$$conversion\ rate\ \% = \frac{amount\ of\ actions\ \#}{impressions\ \#} \times 100\%$$

This is it on the topic of KPI. I believe I've achieved what I've set out to do and I'm sure everybody has understood the difference between a measure and calculated values (KPIs). If you're looking for a perfect set of marketing KPIs, I strongly recommend for you to read the book from Mark Jeffery about the 15 most important marketing metrics (Jeffery, 2010).

Trends

As mentioned above, most measures and KPIs will be time-dependent. One of the most confusing aspects of this is digging into the details of this dimension. Within our experiment, we measured the numbers every minute, thus all our pictures now show a clear timestamp each increased by a minute. Our whiteboard always shows the updated total amount of each measure.

Comparing two historic pictures gives us the delta in-/decrease per measure by an easy subtraction of the same measure gathered at two different points in time. Similar to the KPIs, we can calculate the number of impressions per day, week, month, or year by selecting the correct first and last picture and calculate the delta of both measured amounts. Often, the distribution of these deltas over a timescale is much more interesting than the total amount per timestamp. The first derivation (this is what a physicist would call this) intuitively shows the speed we increase/decrease a measure. While the increase of impressions per day is low at the beginning and end of our campaign, we face a peak in the middle of our timeframe. The picture below on the right illustrates the first derivation. As you can see, it's much better than just showing the pure trendline of the total amount of impression over a time axis (left picture).

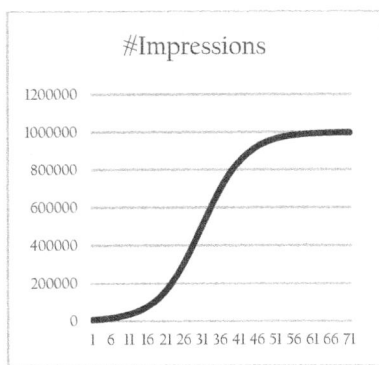
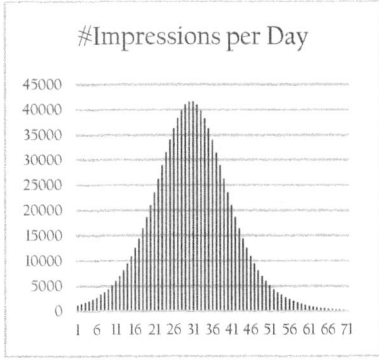

The left chart clearly shows that over a timeframe of 70 days, we had 1 million impressions (gross reach#). But to see how many impressions we had per day, we would need to build the first derivation and count the difference between two consecutive days. The second chart tells us that around day 28–32, we've put bold pressure on the market by adding more than 40,000 impressions a day. It's easy to imagine using the same calculation metric for impressions per week or month.

To summarize this, even if our wall only has dedicated snapshots with timestamps, we can still use this information to show distributions over time and calculate per day, week, month, and year values. This is done by interpolation between two snapshots and aggregation across multiple of them.

Aggregated KPIs of unique

But is this true for all measures? Think about the net reach# we defined above; to reiterate, the measure shows us the number of unique people who caught a ball in our experiment. At this point, the pictures of our whiteboards don't help much. Yes, they show the total number of people, but we can't count per day, week, or month like this.

Why? Let us dig a bit deeper here. If I caught a ball on the first day, you would count me as one unique person. Even if I catch more balls on the following days, I'm still just one unique person, and the system doesn't increase the total amount of net reach#. Let's assume I've caught a second and third ball on days 2 and 3, and nobody else has caught any balls these days. This means the total net reach # for the first three days is still one. If we now switch over to a net reach# per day and use our previous metric, this means it was one for the first day and none for the second and third. But hey, this doesn't reflect the reality; on a per-day scale, we have one unique each day, which means one unique person has caught a ball. It looks like we need to handle these types of unique measures and KPIs differently. You can't aggregate or split them in the way we do this with the pure counts of gross amounts. First, you need to define the timeslot and, then measure the number of unique people within this cell.

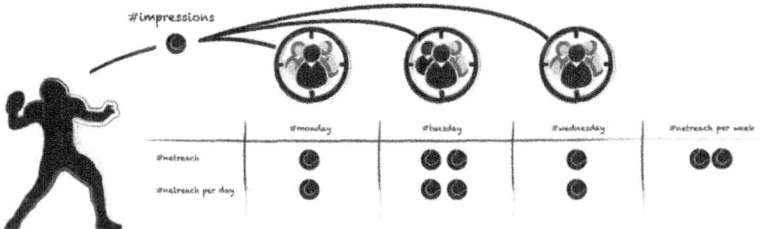

To cut this long story short, the same principles need to be applied in case we enhance our experiment and introduce further dimensions — like differently colored balls and throwing techniques.

Audience centric KPI systems

As stated in the paragraphs above, there's a huge difference in the amount of data for the two cases: counting aggregated amounts of impressions per campaign, or counting single events caused by the single individuals within a campaign.

Thus, be cautious! At the moment, we add further complexity to the math behind it, and it very quickly shows us there are limitations — even in a modern data world.

There was a time, I remember, that one of the client team members mentioned in a marginal note that they also like to show unique amounts (we called them audience-centric) beside their currently presented gross KPIs (content-centric, as you just count the content presented, and not the unique audience behind it) in the newly designed dashboards. He also showed me a few impressive and shiny mockups made in Photoshop and PowerPoint. I was super impressed but all my alarm bells started ringing in my head. So, I took the colleague aside to complete a short exercise, which I'm going to share with you here.

The dashboard was delivered worldwide, and the single regions were grouped into countries, areas, continents, and regional headquarters, etc. In total, we had 250 entries in this first tree structure.

The company had more than 300 programs and campaigns in their master data; each country prepared around 150 per year, on average. The final landing page has been tested in A/B tests, thus there were normally on average 3 URLs for each campaign. To cut a long story short, we had several other dimensions in the dashboard: the actions on the landing page, a paid, owned and earned split including the viral increases by sharing effects, devices of the user, etc. (Don't worry, I will explain them in my next Gedankenexperiment 2.0 further below.)

Finally, the user could select the timeframe with the variable sliders to decide the start and end date for the period they liked to analyze. Why is this so complex in an audience-centric world? If we just count content-centric values like impressions or clicks, it's an easy exercise, to sum up, the single amounts per day on-the-fly when you change the filters. But now, if we add audience-centric measures, like Reach1+ or unique clicks, we face a different challenge. If I click on a landing page on a Monday, on a Tuesday, and on a Sunday, these are three clicks but also only one unique click for the week or one for the month and the same for the year. This means every single cell on a timescale and also each of the stints (start/end) has to be measured separately as explained above. In the example of my client, we aligned that we would like to propose single days, weeks, month, and year, plus the possibility of 1st of Jan to a defined free selected date — only this dimension sums up to a total of 795 entries. Last but not least, the dashboard showed a funnel of six measures, such as impressions, clicks, visits, the video started, 50%, 80%, and full view.

What are the effects on our brilliant dashboard by this move towards unique net measures, and KPIs? To provide the data in a realistic user-friendly time, all cells need to be measured and stored in a 'data lake.' An online calculation out of the user interaction logs that keep the single user events, takes with the latest cloud-based, and scalable data centers hours to be calculated on-the-fly — it's similar to the way we do this with gross measures (impressions and clicks) — so pre-calculation is a must-have here.

If you ask yourself why — then here are the easy mathematics behind. We need to measure all the possible combinations of our n-dimensional data cube that we've defined above. This is 250 regions * 150 avg. campaigns * 3 URLs * 6 actions * 3 for paid, owned earned * 2 for viral effects * 50 devices * 795 time periods * 6 measures = 973.652.404.764 cells to be saved and shown in different dashboards. To pre-calculate, nearly 1 trillion data points for the new audience-centric dashboard was an eye-opener and we started tackling the audience topic slightly differently. I will come back to this later in this book.

You should learn from this example that we need to clearly distinguish the measures we're allowed to aggregate and easily use within new calculated KPIs, and the "other world" of audience-centric ones is where we need to be very careful. Aggregation by summing up the amounts over timeframes or other dimensions is not allowed!

Normally, it's at this point that all my clients and participants become aware of the reason why that tiny step from counting impressions towards dealing with single events per unique person is a huge step, in the underlying process, and technology. By steering away from measuring amounts and using them later in an aggregated dashboard, new technologies allow us to store the single interaction within every touchpoint we have with our customers. The use of big data is a must-have in data-driven marketing and enforces enablement and change on all layers — from strategy through processes, towards the organization, and underlying platforms.

State of the art data management platforms (DMP) and customer database platforms (CDP) rely on the storage of log-files that include every single interaction. Here, millions and billions of data records per day are generated and stored in high performing data clusters, based on the newest big data technologies.

This is a fundamental shift; we are turning away from the good old days of web tracking, by counting impressions and clicks without any relationship with who's behind them. But this also implies we are turning away from the ability to gain all the information with a short click of a button. Even the best performing IT platforms of the world aren't able to aggregate nearly 1 trillion data clusters in the example shown above, purely on-the-fly. Instead, we need to pre-calculate the combinations that are interesting for us, by adding queries to the system and run them regularly to aggregate all of the amounts out of the stored user interaction logs.

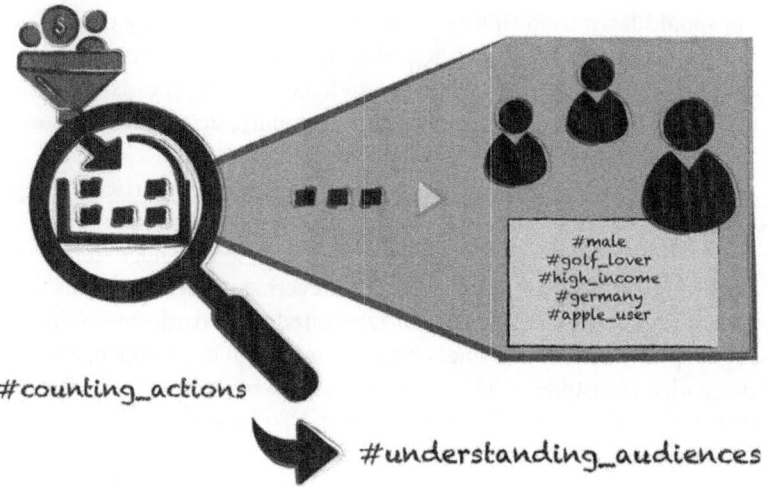

What you should learn from those last paragraphs is that modern, intelligent data-driven marketing, is based on single interactions that can be attributed to unique individuals. This allows us to attribute each interaction within a customer journey towards the intermediate or final action that we'd planned for a dedicated audience.

Without the investment and enablement of the marketing organization to deal with these kinds of audience-centric setups, we will rest in the world of aggregated and context centric marketing data. This level of maturity enables you to growth-hack your business; real data-driven environments allow you to understand your prospects, customers, and all other audiences.

Integrated Reach — a bit of both

There are good reasons for both worlds, the super precise but resource intensive audience centric and the fast and easy context centric world. We also should be aware, that there are some channels like TV, Radio or wallet gardens in digital like most social networks that do not allow to track single user interactions and only provide aggregated numbers.

As reach is the fundamental source to power our marketing funnel we need a formula to monitor our audience across all activation channels and touchpoints. There are different ways and formulas to do this, for me the most prominent is still the Sainsbury formula for integrated marketing reach (Sagovsky, 1963).

This forumal has been invented in Britain for the purpose of estimating reach across channels. The Sainsbury method assumes that exposure is a Bernoulli process (that is, that it follows a binomial distribution). The method can be stated as follows: Rm = 1 - (1 - p1) (1 - p2) (1 - p3) ... (1 - pm) where: Rm = reach of "m" vehicles in a schedule with one insertion in each vehicle. pi = the audience of vehicle "i" expressed as a percentage of the target market size.

As an example let's assume we have: Television reach 65%, Digital Video reach 23% and Social Video reach 34%. Based on the formula above we can calculate the following integrated reach.

Integrated Online Video Reach:

$$video\ online\ reach\ \% = 1 - (1 - social\ video\ reach) * (1 - digital\ video\ reach)$$

$$video\ online\ reach\ \% = 1 - (1 - 34\%) * (1 - 23\%) = 49\%$$

Integrated Video Reach:

$$video\ reach\ \% = 1 - (1 - 34\%) * (1 - 23\%) * (1 - 65\%) = 82\%$$

Smart KPI — Reporting, Dashboarding and Data Science

I think besides the math behind-the-scenes, I should mention that, in all the data-driven marketing projects I've finished on various customer floors, the change management of handling audience-centric KPIs was always a tough endeavor. It's necessary to allow marketing departments to bid farewell to the historic way they consumed data. In most cases, there's sophisticated reporting in place, which allows them to share a massive amount of static reports across the organization to keep everybody informed — from country marketing managers and agencies, via the marketing specialist, up to the headquarter management and CMO.

Pillar 1: Standard Reporting

In audience-centric worlds, this descriptive sharing of standard reports is still one pillar of the data management strategy. Pre-calculated KPIs are mixed up in dashboards together, alongside the easy content-centric ones. This helps everyone to stay on top of the daily operations in the marketing department, as we've done this in the past, from the beginning of madmen marketing.

Pillar 2: Explorative Data Analytics

The introduction of more ways to deal with the data is new within mathman marketing. The first method, a diagnostic method, is a more explorative way of using the data; it allows us to slice and dice the provided data. Fixed data cubes are used in modern data visualization tools, and allow us to find more details, and generate individual dashboards and graphs by the easy drag and drop method. These dashboards and stories are often shared collaboratively, via the organization and discussed within several groups. This means this second data and analytics pillar enhances the standard reports by exploration and collaboration across a defined set of structured and pre-calculated data.

Pillar 3: Data Science

The third pillar of modern data management is the introduction of data science within your organization. Highly specialized scientists use the data to discover underlying patterns through different models. This allows them to glance into the future, to predict the behavior and next steps of your customers. Data Scientists use a broad range of algorithms for this, starting with easy regressions and clusters — ultimately ending up with a complex chain analysis and decision trees.

    The trade-off is that we need to stop using our preferred self-service way of using reports, dashboards, and explorative data cubes. Instead, organizations need to learn how the leverage central data science capabilities. Normally this is done via a workflow of postulating a hypothesis that describes the effect and cause of a single topic. This topic is what you assume has happened in the real world. The final proof is done by the scientist, with a deep dive into the underlying big data world and the use of algorithms. So, people need to learn how to request the data science support through a hypothesis, and data scientists must learn how to deliver efficient results in an agile project environment.

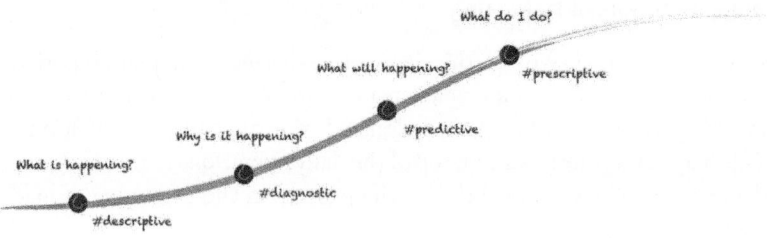

To be completely honest, I must mention the fourth pillar: the prescriptive world. Here, exact models and algorithms allow us to describe complex systems and fully simulate them, based on formulas and mathematics instead of predictive algorithms. I'm more than convinced that marketing and the underlying behavior of customers are far away from being described in a prescriptive model as we see in every physical discipline. We'll never find some magical formula, like $e=m*c^2$ that helps us to deliver perfect marketing. But as a certified physicist, I'm still fascinated by the idea of finding algorithms instead of patterns, that allow us to dig deeper into the cause and effect relationships of complex systems.

Later on, in this book, after explaining a more sophisticated and closer-to-reality Gedankenexperiment 2.0, I'm going to use some physical theories and link them to marketing. This will give us real mathematical frameworks and algorithms that help to set up sophisticated predictive models.

Gedankenexperiment 2.0

After we reduced the complexity and kept it to a minimum in our first lab setup and system of reference, I would like to use a second experiment to add in some complexity, but in a pre-defined way. Instead of analyzing all possible variations and the latest trends in marketing, the virtual lab allows us to pick and choose just one topic and think about the possible enhancements and their implications.

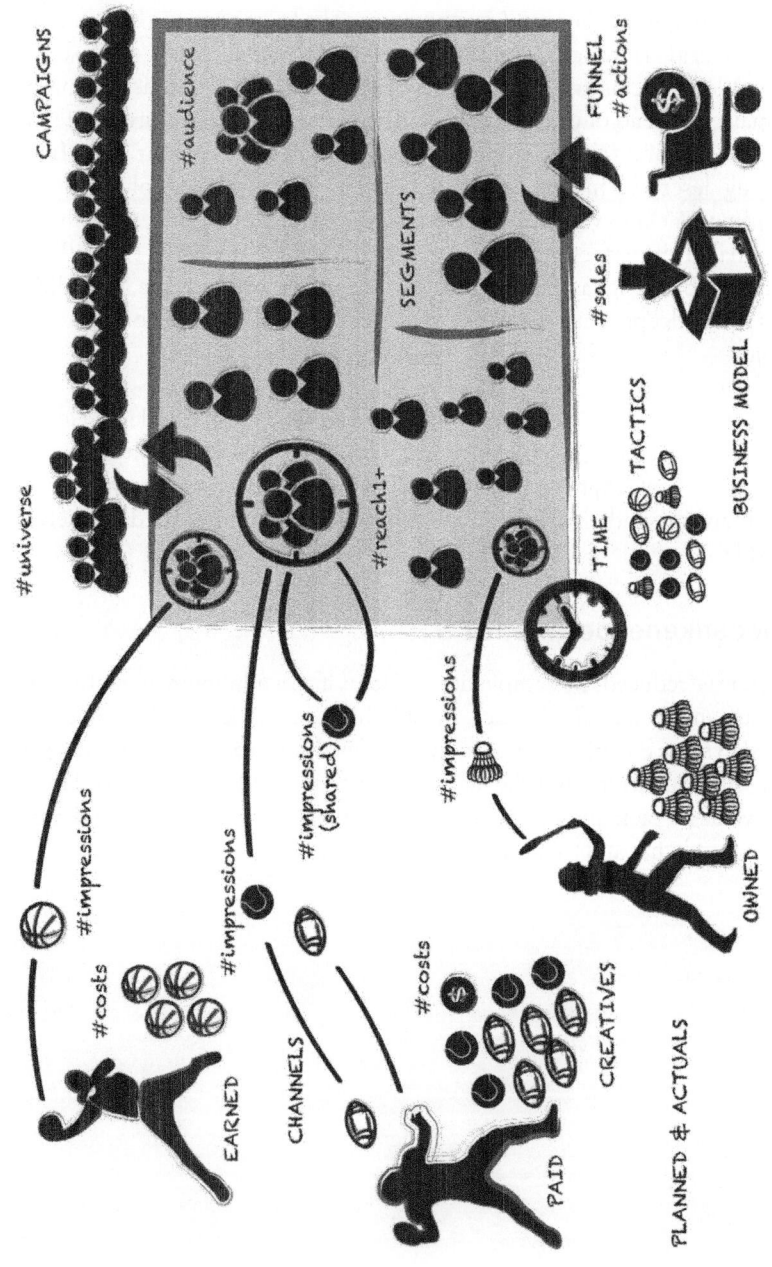

A house is not enough — strategic marketing planning

In our first experiment, we've just defined one house as the room of interaction that we have with our counterparts — to keep it simple, let's call them "customers." However, for simulating the real world, this may be too simple. It's obvious that in every large marketing department, we will find multiple campaigns running at the same time.

Drawing back to our imaginary lab, this means that we are no longer active within the square and under the roof of one single house. Instead, we populate a full city within a region and dedicated country borders with audiences, people throwing balls, and others writing amounts on our whiteboards.

Unique Identifiers

What are the side effects that we should consider? First of all, the audience is no longer distinct and clear as it was in our 1.0 version of the experiment. People can walk from one house to the other, and they will enter the room with a half-filled basket of balls. To get the right numbers, especially the audience-centric ones, we need to mark everybody we hit with a ball, who caught a ball, and those who bought a basket. To do this, we introduce a new player to the game a tiny micro dino into each house. Let's call him "Saffi Chrozilla." He has one task only, and that is to put a cookie into the pocket of every member of the audience once he enters our house. It's a magic cookie because the melted chocolate core has a special flavor with a unique smell. Whenever we want to identify one of our customers, we need the gatekeeper dinosaurs in the houses to sniff the cookie out with their keen sense of smell. They'll tell us the unique smell in the form of a unique number code — and that's it. Now, we can write down every interaction mapped against this code on our whiteboards. We make the field of action easy by collecting aggregated amounts on our whiteboard and enter the world of intelligent, data-driven marketing by collecting every single interaction mapped against a unique number.

Central Data Management and Customer Data Platforms

However, still, we face the problem that once somebody leaves our houses and crosses the street to the next house, we are running blind. The second group of ball thrower, dino, and whiteboard artist is not aware of what's happened in the first house. Though, this can be solved easily; the solution is to interconnect all the houses. We increase our velocity by taking pictures of the whiteboard every second and immediately send them to a central office that shares all the consolidated information gained out of all deliveries and send it to each house. If someone enters a new house, the dino will identify the new smell and instead of adding a new cookie into the pocket, the dino reaches out to the central office. There, he gets the latest information of the customer, all stored in the lake of consolidated data sheets sent by all houses.

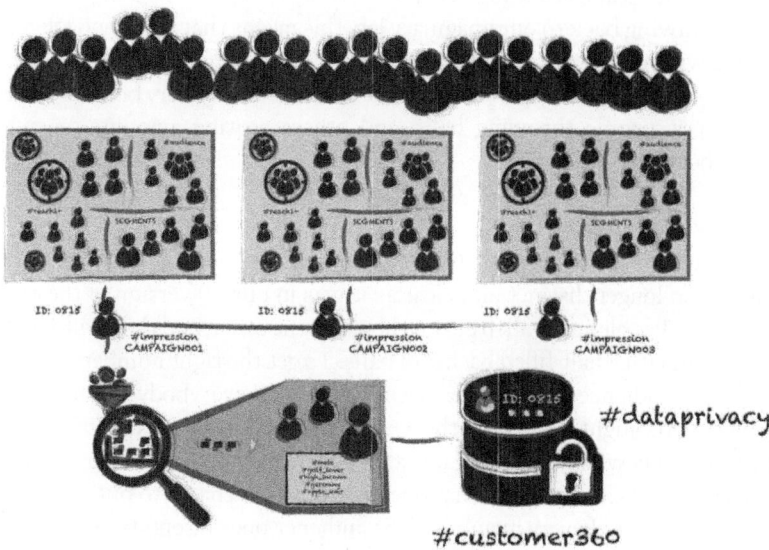

Strategic Campaign Portfolio Planning

Last but not least, we should take into consideration, that the sheer number of houses that our audience can enter may confuse them. And, of course, it's reasonable to assume that we would attempt to optimize the number of balls we buy upfront. Within the 1.0 experiment, we could easily estimate the maximum number of balls we needed by using the basket sizes, hit accuracy, and the size of the target audience. But for 2.0, it's not as simple now; we need to first find a balance for the number of balls we need per house, the target audiences, tactical segments we would like to reach, the time we like to open the house doors, etc. This means we need to include a process for strategic upfront planning and a continuous feedback loop so we hit our plans.

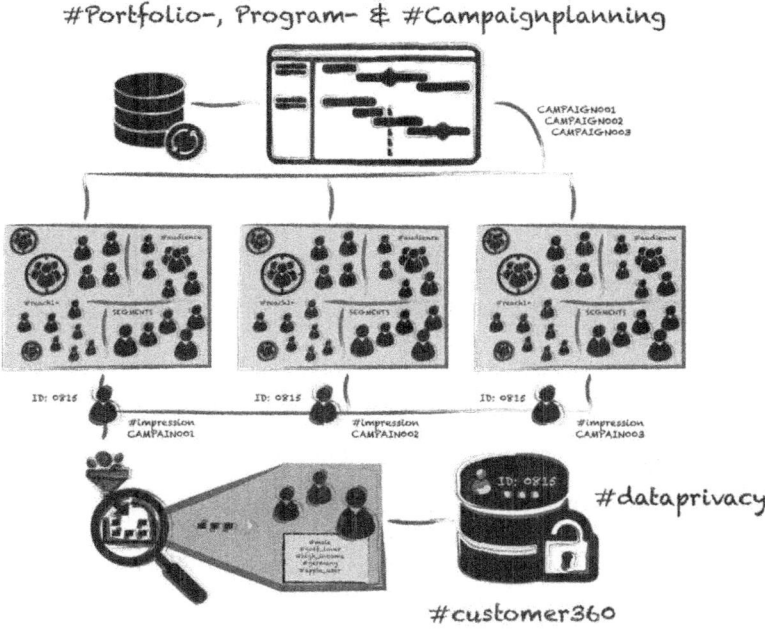

To conclude, by increasing the territory from one house to cities, regions, and countries, we see three implications we need to focus on: first, there is the need to have unique identifiers in the form of unique cookies and a central repository to share them amongst all in the game; secondly, we need a central entity overarching all of our houses, cities, and regions, which is where everything comes together. The central office can host the central data management and customer data platform and shares further information based on requests. Furthermore, it can push out a defined set of information regularly; thirdly, a planning workflow needs to be implemented which allows us to distribute the number of balls we purchase per house, and to control where we are in comparison to the original plan.

Another interesting piece of information you can learn from our first enhancement to the basic experiment 1.0 is from looking at the measures, KPIs, and dimensions of the new setup 2.0. We still don't increase the number of possible measures we had in 1.0, but we have introduced a new set of dimensions.

As well as this, we've introduced special processes and platforms to run our 2.0 experiment. The campaign preparation and execution process we have described in our previous Gedankenexperiment is no longer sufficient, and the planning of a full-blown portfolio of programs and campaigns has been added.

Process and Rules	Organization
• Strategic marketing planning • Interconnected homes → multi-campaign preparation and execution	• A **striker** who throws the balls • Data Analyst who fills the whiteboard • **Central** Data Team who handles the different data requests
Platforms	Data and Dimension
• Central lake of Audience Profiles/data sheets → DMP and CDP • Campaign planning, preparation and controlling system → marketing resource management within a marketing cloud • The gatekeeper dinos → tag management system	• The name of the cities, regions, and countries → marketing programs, plans, and brands.

Different Balls — creative management & optimization

Moving away from the overall setup, let's focus more on the individual houses and what happens inside them. Playing the full game within all houses and cities with one ball is far too simplistic. In the real marketing world, we see a huge variety of visuals (creatives and branded content) that are used to attract different target audiences. Most of them are tailored to the way we communicate with our customers, and their moods and feelings. In our experiment, we will see within the following chapters if this correlates with the way we best throw our balls towards the tactical segments. But before looking at ball throwing techniques, we should enhance our Gedankenexperiment 2.0 with the possibility of easier customization with different forms and colors for our balls.

Creative & Content Management (Marketing Assets)

While the form is more related to the format we can use (i.e. static banners, moving images in digital, tv and cinema, printed posters in and out of home environments, etc.), the color is more about the propensity of the audience members to catch a ball and add them to their basket. For example, blue may work better for one of our tactical segments and red better for the other.

A/B Testing

To find out what works best, we first need to throw both colors towards both tactical segments. After the first iteration, we should go back to our whiteboard and check the number of thrown balls (impression), balls put into the customer's basket (conversions), and attribute these values to the form, color, and tactical segment our striker used.

Dynamic Creative Optimization

It's clear that the logistic of buying balls has increased immensely; no longer do we see that just all the houses use the same type of balls. Our planning process now has to consider buying the right color and forms for the different houses and deliver them in time so they're ready when the strategic audiences reach our different houses.

Let's have a closer look at the amendments we've made to our experiment. First, we added different forms and colors, as well as correlated the purchasing, and the logistic process to ship them to the pre-defined locations of our different houses. It appears as if we have an enhancement of our strategic marketing planning. Now, this also includes the definition of "ball demands" and the controlling of the logistic and shipment to the different houses.

Next, we should pay attention to the perfect fit of tactical segments and ball color. In the good old days of mad-men marketing, we would fully rely on our experience. In the new world of data-driven marketing, we run a so-called A/B Test that is split into multiple iterations, and a 'trial and error' approach to see what works well and where there's room for improvements. This only works when the striker, the whiteboard data analyst, and our central data team works perfectly together.

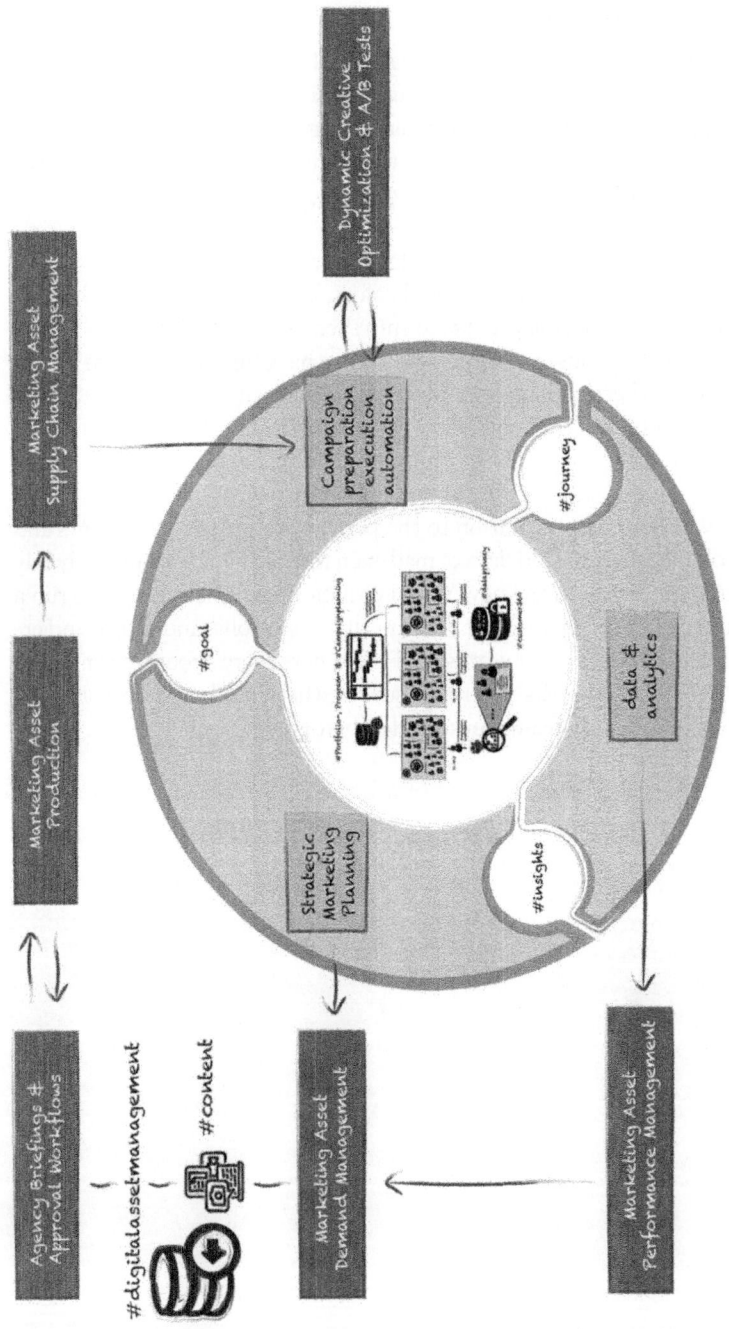

So now, it's time for a short digression away from the main topic. Instead, I want to take you on a (worthwhile) short journey for a sneak preview of what is classed as 'state of the art' in modern marketing — so keep on reading, you'll be surprised at what you'll learn.

If we were to go back to the balls scenario and focus on the vendors who are selling us these balls that we're using. Let's assume one of our vendors is bringing out a new type of ball — it's a completely, brand new, innovative 'super' ball. It's white, but as soon as it crosses the 'catching area' of a possible customer — wow! It changes color. This would work based upon the aroma of our hidden cookies that are placed in the pockets of potential customers. Though, some people differ with how they 'receive' things better; some people are more responsive to audio, while others respond more to visual triggers. The solution to this is to have some of these balls (rather than changing color) will play pleasant music to attract attention. These types of balls are much more expensive than the range of standard ones, but they're worth a try (and the investment into them). A potential plan could be to use them within just one house and, similarly to our A/B test, we will see whether they work. We will also see an increase in more baskets bought. The money made from the extra baskets will, hopefully, be higher than the purchasing price for the new balls, and therefore we would have covered our extra expenses for them. In the marketing world, we call this domain "dynamic creative optimization and branded content". The classic production and organization of the balls is the "creative demand and management process."

Agile Marketing

Optimization is based on testing with trial and error, which can only be carried out in an agile environment that allows it to run fast and fail fast. The execution is split into several sprints with retrospective and re-planning at both ends of an iteration. We will approach the topic, "agile fail fast" approach later as you read further into the book.

We took a two-fold test approach: firstly, we used different colored balls and forms, and secondly, we tested the different types of balls. While the first approach aimed to find the most successful color fit to the audience in small time boxes known as agile sprints or iterations, the second test evaluated something new in only one location to see the results.

70-20-10

This is another fundamental principle of modern data-driven marketing. Use 70% of your resources and budget on known and things for working (balls, throwing techniques, locations, etc.), another 20% should be used to invest into new, but established formats. The last 10% is put into unknown and highly innovative formats, often designed by the advertiser. Until then, they weren't seen somewhere in the marketing ecosystem.

To summarize our mini digression, we have learned a lot (and hopefully you have too) by focusing on different colored balls and adaptively designed balls rather than single-colored balls, and how they could impact potential customers. We faced two new processes: creative management and organization and added several new dimensions to our experiment, such as color, form, and music we played. We also found a new use-case for the tiny cookies we placed in the pockets of our target audiences. And at the end, we learned a new way of working by distributing our budget and resources wisely 70-20-10 and executing in small agile sprints combined with ongoing A/B testing.

Process and Rules	Organization
• Creative & Content Management • Dynamic Creative Optimization and branded content • 70-20-10 Rule • Agile Marketing	• Sprint teams • Creative Production and Delivery
Platforms	Data and Dimension
• Personalization and A/B testing engine • Digital Asset Management to deliver and store content	• Colors and Forms • Sprints • Type of investment (known, new, innovative)

Smaller Segments — hyper-accurate targeting and look-a-likes

The previous chapter focused more on the possibility of tailoring the balls to our tactical segments of tall and medium-sized people. There is no need to know the persons behind it or tag them with a hidden cookie. We just used our eyes and check whether they are taller than 1.70 m and target only them. Now, we're enhancing this approach and making it more sophisticated and we shall include the cookies we placed in each audience member's pocket.

Hyper accurate targeting on 1st party data

Our dinos work incredibly hard on their task to identify each potential customer by the smell of the cookie, and they also work extra hard on other tasks, including observing behaviors, skills, and other attributes to the unique identifiers. This can easily be done by exploring what these peoples are doing: some people may have started using their mobile phones while waiting for balls, let's class them as "smartphone lovers." Others may have coffee and begin making small talk with their neighbors, we class them as "coffee lovers." With this logic, if we waited for longer, then we can collect more data about potential customers just by observing their reactions. While waiting for something, people tend to begin talking to strangers in the line about a lot of things, which includes conversations about their kids ("moms and dads"), and about their hobbies ("motorsport enthusiasts," "surfers," "bikes," and "music lovers"). They may also buy other products offered in our houses, so we could use this information to find out more about their character. There is a group frequently buying health products, another group getting diapers via a frequent abo model, etc. — there are endless possibilities to cluster them down into specific categories. Our cookie, or to be more precise, the unique identifier allows us to define hyper granular audience segments based on the behavior of every single member. In our modern world, we can assign 20 to 30 thousand attributes to each cookie; to classify the data, we call it 1st party data if we collect it ourselves; it becomes 2nd or 3rd party data if our business partners or someone unknown like a social network collected them.

Consent Management and Data Protection

As we abide by the global game rules, we trained our dinos to no longer place the cookies without informing the target audience. Now, large signs at the houses' entrances show entrants what we are planning to do with the collected data. We're friendly, professional and are polite and honest to our audience; it's for this reason that we give them the choice to close the buttons on their pockets so they're not tracked via a unique cookie or to just eat the cookie we placed there before.

Currently, there are ongoing discussions regarding social networks and the amount of data they are gathering from their users; this has, of course, stemmed from Facebook and the Cambridge Analytica case — if you weren't aware, then I would give it a quick search on Google, just so you're in the loop. Now, the methods we're obtaining data, through ball experiments are correct and abides by all data protection rules. Thanks to the strict rules of the European Union (GDPR), the long-time existing grey zone of data handling is more and more regulated and controlled.

Again, I'm going to digress slightly at the end of this chapter — only very briefly, though, on the topic of the data footprints, we leave every day. So, most people who won't know the ins and outs of marketing data or aren't experts in the field don't know that we leave millions of digital footprints every hour (let alone every day) without entering any social network whatsoever. This might be tricky to understand, so I'm going to explain it with a story.

I'm a consultant, which means that I need to travel quite often to reach clients — whether that's by train or plane. On these journeys, how many data points am I'm generating on my way to a client?" My day begins as I'm woken by an app on my smartwatch that monitors the sound of my breathing, and sets off an alarm when it finds the 'perfect' moment to wake me (this would normally be when I'm exiting a deep sleep phase. For this app to work, it needs access to the GPS tool and for it to be activated — I'm not sure why). It collects information on noise, location, and the time you wake up daily, which helps to track your sleeping patterns, so it's a pretty decent app. I've not read all the terms and conditions, so I'm not that aware of the attributes being used in a data-sharing platform. Anyway, let's move on with the day.

As usual, I read my emails first thing so that I can organize my day. There are a few newsletters in my inbox,

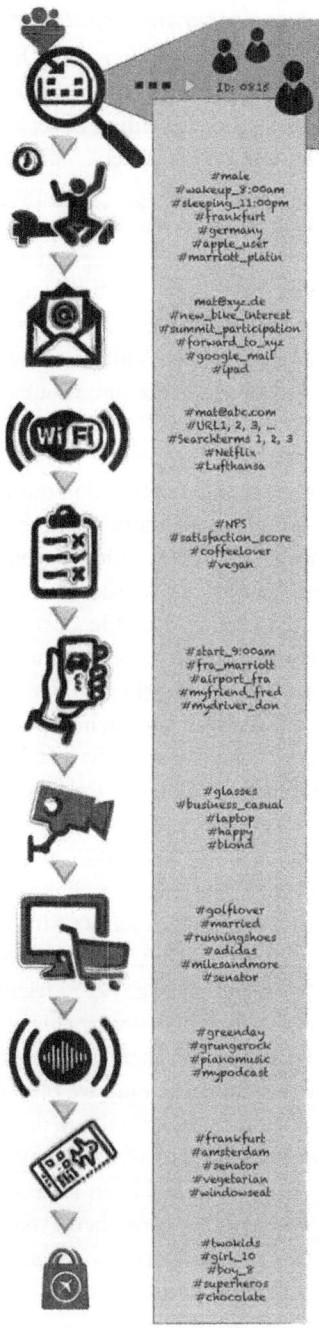

and while I usually don't read them, some of them look interesting, so I had a peak. They'd piqued my interest, so I did begin to read them thoroughly; one seems to be on a topic I believe my colleagues would be interested in, so I forward it onto them. This is a lot of data points, already, and I haven't started the day properly yet. Opened newsletters, forwarded mail, clicked-on content, etc. — these are all stored in the senders of the newsletter's database. In terms of internet connection, I'm connected to the WIFI of the hotel I'm staying in, which requested my email address to subscribe and access the WIFI. However, this is a pretty standard requirement, plus it is free WIFI, so I can't complain. With the hotspot, I hadn't realized before, but it can link all my opened webpages, streams, and the like to my email — I mean, from a technical standpoint it's more than easy to do.

Moving on with my day, I checked out of the hotel and filled in a small survey about my experience on the way out as best I could. I always like to be polite and give good, helpful feedback. This is when I'll need to get a taxi to the airport. Luckily, my friend told me about this great app which makes it more convenient to order a taxi — again, there's a huge amount of data points here. Checking out, the hotel's survey, talking to my friend who shared the app with me, my pick-up location at the hotel, my final destination, time, the bookmarked drivers, etc. I also realized the dashcam in the car that was there for security would be recording me, and I kept thinking about how there's no restriction (technically) on sophisticated image recognition to record me to enable others to find out more about me. Of course, there are terms and conditions on the tiny disclaimer in front of me, as well as within the app, which I accepted without checking thoroughly.

While in the taxi, I decided to finish some online shopping on my tablet and also streamed my favorite playlists via a music streaming portal.

During this short drive, I've provided endless amounts of information — the new device I used, products I've looked on the website, some of them I've put on my 'watch' list, some I bought directly, the music I skipped, the one I heard the first and a second time, etc.

At the airport, I start checking in, including the hand-over of my preferred meal preferences. Finally, I will buy some presents for my kids at the duty-free and opt-in to the offer to collect double miles for each euro I've spent on my airline loyalty program. The trade-off that they are allowed to collect single line item data on my credit card buys is something I accept, with an easy click on the "Allow All" button during the subscription — who reads those terms and conditions anyway?

I think you can imagine how this story proceeds. There's no escape from leaving digital data footprints. It's up to us to be aware of this and take care that we check and maintain the sharing opt-ins we give to the platforms thoroughly and start learning how to live within a data-driven world.

Look-a-like on 2nd and 3rd party data

Now that's out of the way, let's circle back around to my topic of hyper-accurate targeting. We've now seen how many attributes we leave as digital footprints. Our team that throws the balls is now taking care of this, instead of just distinguishing between the tall- and medium-sized, they start segmenting their audience on 1st, 2^{nd,} and 3rd party data into hundreds of tactical segments. Through a large amount of A/B testing, they find out what the best fitting ball forms and colors are for each one of these segments. Conversions in the form of a ball put to the basket are rising by a factor of 10 for the best working segments — what a great success!

But this is only half of our story, we could be even more efficient by leveraging the segments built on 1st party data and showing the highest conversions. Instead of further testing and losing balls on non-performing segments, we'll focus on throwing them in the best working ones and neglect the rest. Soon, we will see all baskets are full and people becoming stressed because the balls are flying around. It looks like we've just run into a dilemma. The more data we have coming in, our segments increase accuracy, but the tradeoff is that the size of our audience decreases. If we still want to throw the complete set of balls we paid for upfront, we don't have enough reach of people in our highly performing tactical segments.

One possible solution would be a magic crystal ball newly installed in the central office on top of our data management and customer data platform, with two new pipes connected to it. The first allows us to buy additional marketing attributes for profiles (cookie IDs) we already have within our lake through previous campaigns. The second pipe allows us to buy completely new profiles to increase the total amount of planned reach in the central lake.

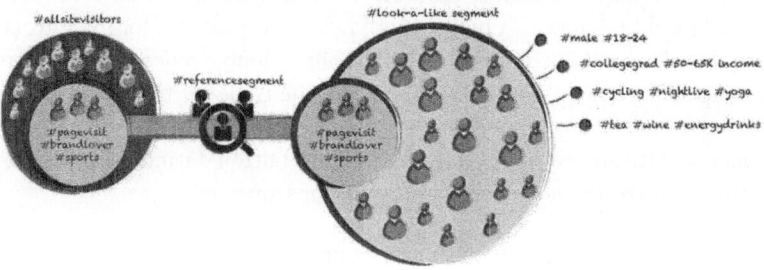

Both cases force us to change the rules of "campaign execution" that we're playing within our houses. Now, we first fill the rooms with a tiny test group, build hyper-accurate target groups by massively using our own collected attributes out of previous campaigns (1st party data). To be more accurate, we open one of the pipes and enhance our profiles with additional attributes for each of our profiles in the lake (2nd and 3rd party data attributes). The new setup enables us to choose between thousands of different marketing attributes, which helps with tailoring the segments perfectly. Now, we run a first round of throwing balls against these segments to identify the ones that work ones. An analysis of the segment's performances is how this sprint will end.

To avoid stressing out the people we'd stressed out previously with their filled baskets, we need to increase the reach of people before starting the second sprint. Instead of just opening the doors to everyone for this second round of throwing balls, we use the second pipe and open it to blow up our number of profiles mapped against new IDs (2nd and 3rd party data profiles).

Programmatic Marketing

Our predictive crystal ball analyzes our best working segments in the first test sprint. Based on the millions of attributes, it can build clusters and find similar profiles in the data lake; the name of the game is "find look-a-likes." Instead of now leaving the entrance open to everybody, the dinos take care that only the people we've identified in our "look-a-like" segments can enter the room. The result is a campaign that runs on similar segment sizes compared to our experiment 1.0, with the difference that the likelihood they'll catch a ball is 10 times higher. Welcome to the world of predictive and programmatic marketing!

I'm sure your brain is now running on maximum power. This chapter of hyper-accurate targeting includes a whole host of amazing information, tips, and tricks to help increase the efficiency and effectiveness of our marketing campaigns. It also cuts the edge of integrity and legitimacy of working with customer data and the necessity to stay in line with clear game rules, like the general data protection rules of different countries.

Finally, I'd like to wrap up the amendments of our experiment and define new processes, and necessary platform enhancements. Not only have we seen the possibility to collect 1st part data for better targeting within clear rules of given consent by the single customer, but we've seen the trade-off of stressed audiences and a frequency cap, the predictive solution of enhancing the segment reach by look-a-like modeling also on shared 2nd and 3rd party data and profiles, and finally, a way to control the people reached in our houses via programmatic marketing.

Process and Rules	Organization
• Hyper Accurate Targeting • Frequency Management • Look-a-like Modelling • Programmatic Marketing • Data Protection Management	• Data Protection Manager • Audience Specialist • Programmatic Specialist
Platforms	Data and Dimension
• Data Sharing Platforms for 2rd and 3rd party data • Predictive Data Management and Customer Data Enhancements and Frameworks	• Consent Status • With the connection to the 2nd and 3rd party data market, the amount of dimension we now can use is depending on the data-sharing platform we use, and what they can provide. As said above 20 to 30 thousand attributes per cookie can be bought on the current data sharing market.

Multiple Players — paid, owned, earned

Returning to our Gedankenexperiment 2.0, we're still relying on one person throwing the balls towards our target audiences. As he's part of our team, we don't need to pay him any salaries or fees to do this. I'd like to label him for that reason as "owned." because he is part of our core team.

Paid, owned and earned marketing

But there are other possibilities than "being owned." It's certain that throwing balls and hitting the right people is a discipline other people can train themselves so they can provide that service to the market. Thus, we could reach out to this group called *"marketing networks and agencies."* We can enhance our velocity of throwing balls by engaging people from these networks. However, there's a trade-off, just like last time; we need to pay additional money to the new striker that I'm going to label as "paid." In the real world, there's much more value by using these networks. They also provide services that help to optimize the setup of your city, houses, balls, etc. I will come to this later on in the book.

The Imaginary Marketing Lab

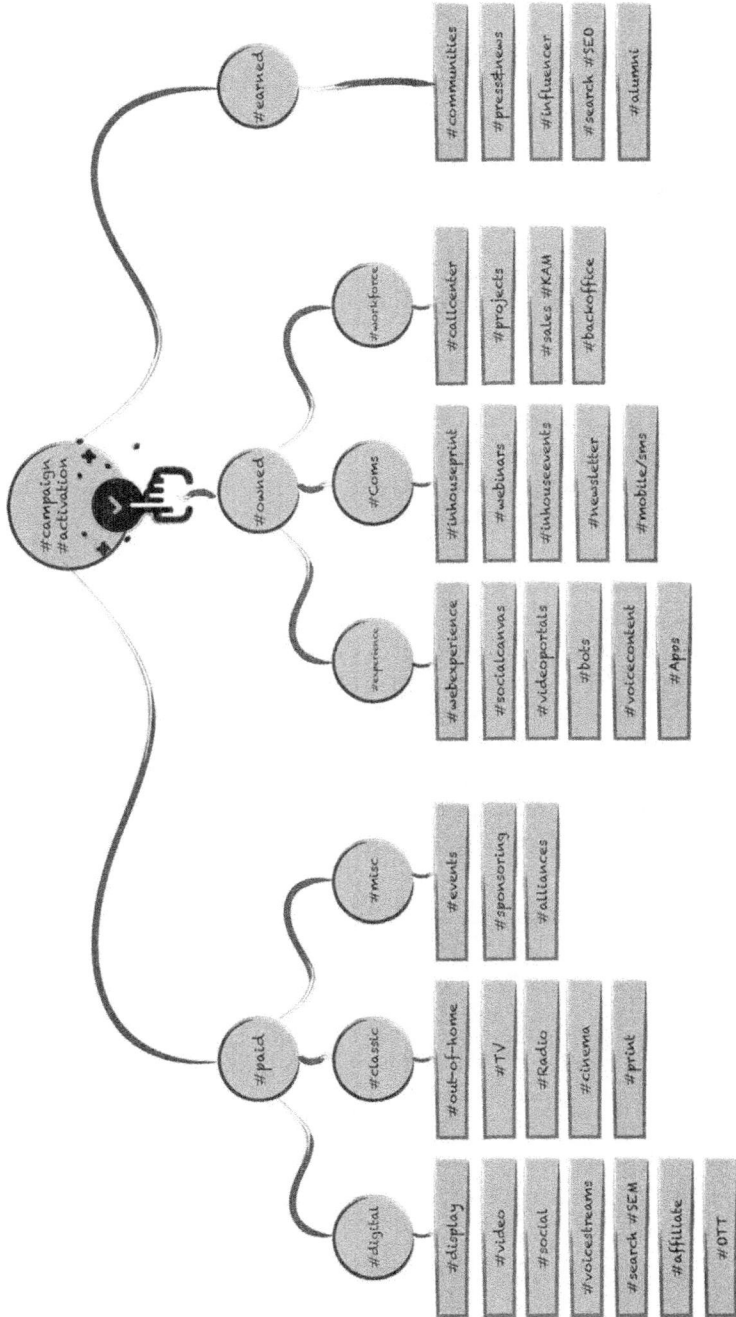

Alongside "paid" and "owned," there's a third group we may like to add to our lab setup. It's possible to motivate dedicated people to throw balls for us without paying them, which means they'll essentially do it for fun. Or better yet, we just piggyback our message on their balls and whenever they throw them towards their audiences, a bit of our message is also put out for the customers to read.

In the real world, we're talking about press releases, the content we post on our partner networks, cross-linking on their internet portals, mentions within their video blogs, etc. All the additional hits we achieve through these new strikers are for free; I call these "earned."

Distributed Campaign Execution

It's time to delve deeper into our lab set up, and the type of implications the enhancement through paid and earned teams have resulted in. I think the first is quite obvious — it gives our strategic marketing plan another layer of complexity. Now we've broadened our scope and increased our teams, we need to factor in all paid (and if possible) earned team players into our planning. Everyone needs to be trained like our original team in how to tackle our audiences specifically. As they have their own central offices, we need to find a way of syncing their collected information into our central storage. If they use spiders or other tiny animals to place their cookies, then a "cookie sync" needs to be established, otherwise, we won't be able to identify whom they might have thrown a ball to and if the customer has put it in his basket. A joined frequency cap on paid, owned, and earned teams needs to be established as well. The "network and agency management" is a fully new process that needs to be added to our scope.

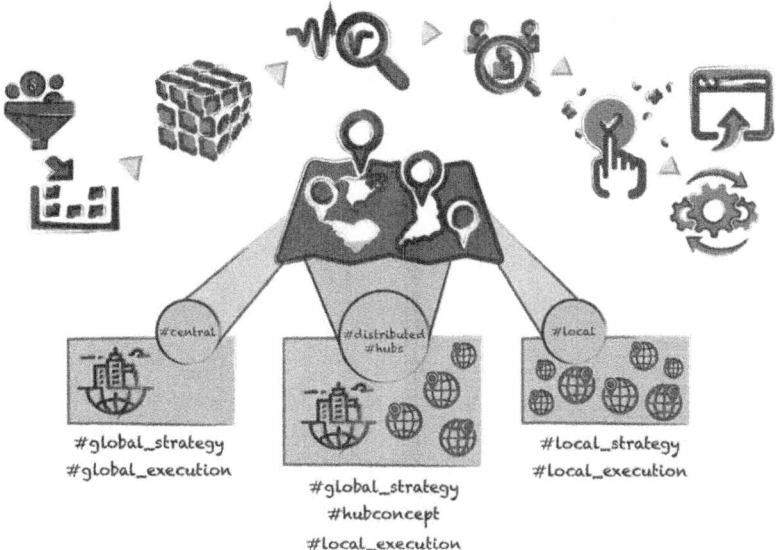

Marketing Partner & Agency Management

We would also like to avoid them storing data on their systems so they can use it later in other houses (campaigns), which is why there needs to be a strict contract in place. The authorities also put rules in place on how to store and use personal data within our ecosystem, thus we need to be sure they also follow all these rules. Again, GDPR and other data protection rules is a huge topic right now in modern society. Alongside the layer of complexity we added by increasing the organization and system, we also add a layer of costs with paid and earned teams. The fees and activation costs from our paid team need to be considered and tracked on the whiteboard in the back of our rooms. Since pricing is always a type of creative art, there are several models in place. The most common is to "pay per use," — the partner charges us a tiny surplus for every thousand balls they throw into the room. As described above, this is the calculated KPI and it's called CPM (cost per mille). Other models use the metric of caught balls (CTR) or any other action (cost per action/CPA). On top of this, in most cases, there's an additional fixed fee in the form of a percentage of the activation cost, the total amount per campaign, or the timeframe charged by the partner. By summarizing the new paid and earned striker teams, we see the need for a distributed marketing model. As we deal with new external parties, strict agency management needs to be established.

Process and Rules	Organization
• Marketing Partner Management • Cost Planning and Management	• Data Protection Manager • Audience Specialist • Programmatic Specialist
Platforms	Data and Dimension
• Distributed Marketing Planning Platform • Finance and Controlling Platform	• Paid, owned and earned classifications • Different Cost layers

Throwing tactics — the media mix and attribution models

With the advent of new strikers in our game, we should start considering two further things: the technique we use to throw the balls into the room and the time, dimension, and sequences of throwing a series of balls.

Media Channel Mix Optimization

Let's have a closer look at our paid, owned, and earned striker teams; each of them can push and throw our balls in various ways. The paid striker has a few classic ways of throwing slightly to the top of the room in a curve, instead of straight powerful shots to the target audience. He can also do it like a French "boule gamer" by taking the ball into his whole hand and facing the back of his hand towards the target audience. The owned striker is also trained but doesn't want to tell us if, how, and when he is throwing the balls. This is also fine but it's more difficult to count on him and his different tactics. On the positive side, it looks like we've enhanced our model with various ways to reach our audience — the perfect mix will increase our conversion massively!

Returning to our experiment and enhancements for 2.0 above, I'd like to repeat the fact that we've placed unique cookies in the pockets of our audiences and stored all interactions in central data management and customer data platform. Now, instead of randomly giving the striker team the ability to throw their balls, we can rely on a different approach. The current standard is to always use just one set of techniques. But we can implement a round-robin with a defined one after one sequence of a dedicated technique, or we could take advantage of the data we collected in previous games.

By analyzing a large amount of data and use the same pattern as above by testing the combination of different techniques in A/B tests, we can identify the most successful throwing tactics. We would start testing different combinations to reach our target audiences in a short sprint. The difference to the above-described test is that success is defined by the amount of caught balls per mix of thrown balls. The conversion of just a single shot is no longer taken into consideration. Within the following sprint (the second one) we put more money and effort into the most successful combination of striker shots, while continually testing new combinations that might be the winner for sprint three, four, five, etc., with a tiny share of our budget.

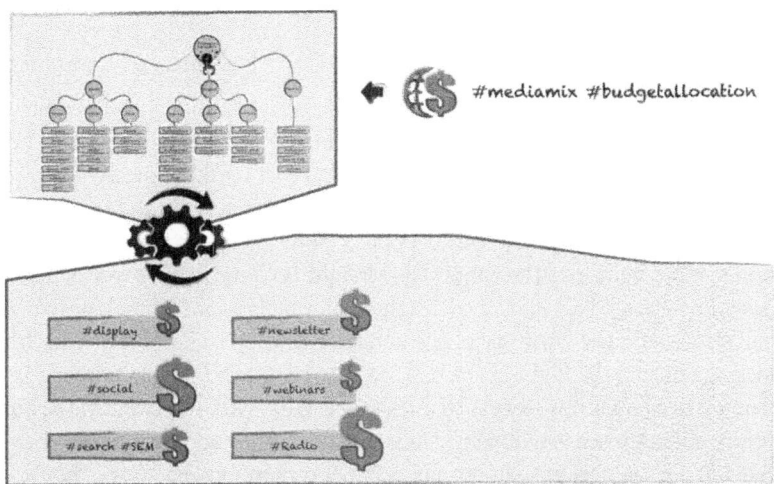

Attribution Models

In this first optimization, we focused on the mix of different throwing techniques without really taking considering the time, only the mix of techniques was used for conversion optimization. It was more of a way to find out the budget balance of how much we should allocate to which throwing technique. We worked on this perfect balance; in the real marketing world, we call this media mix optimization. The mix is a powerful way to screw up the conversion and success of our striker team. But wait, there's more! It's time to think about the second optimization possibility — the time dimension and sequence of throwing techniques.

Again, our cookies come into the game. While the mix was just counting the ratio of how often we used different techniques, we could reach out to our central office and connect to their data management and customer data platform. Every player gets a new task; he needs to transmit the information of who he tried to hit and he does this by combining the unique production number of the thrown ball with the way he pushed it out, and the unique identifier of our cookie in the pocket of his target. This information is, again, stored in our central office with the big data lake, and has an exact timestamp. Now we can build a full path of interactions we've had with each participant in our target audience. If we also collect all the other actions like catching the ball, putting it to a basket, etc., together with the unique cookie ID into our lake, we can analyze the conversions based on the sequence of actions. Then, we can model a customer journey within a pre-defined marketing funnel, which is a concept I will explain in the next chapter.

We will find out that our initial conversion rate is not influenced by solely the last actions. Let us assume a straight, boldly thrown ball showed the highest conversion. The logical consequence is that we attributed this technique to the highest likelihood that our target segment will catch a ball and put it into his basket. If we were to take a closer look into the sequence, it brings more light into the game. The straight bold move only works if we have thrown two balls upfront with the "boule technique." This slow-flying ball stimulated the curiosity of the audience as they could partly read the message during the flight of the ball crossing their head. The hypothesis is, that we need some awareness that there are balls with a message in the air before our audience is willing to catch the balls. So, by adding more interactions in a sequence, we can optimize and add more budget to the "boule > boule > straight" variant. The "straight > straight > straight" technique shows a pure performance in comparison. Again, we optimized the conversion by analyzing sequences of throwing techniques instead of the pure mix.

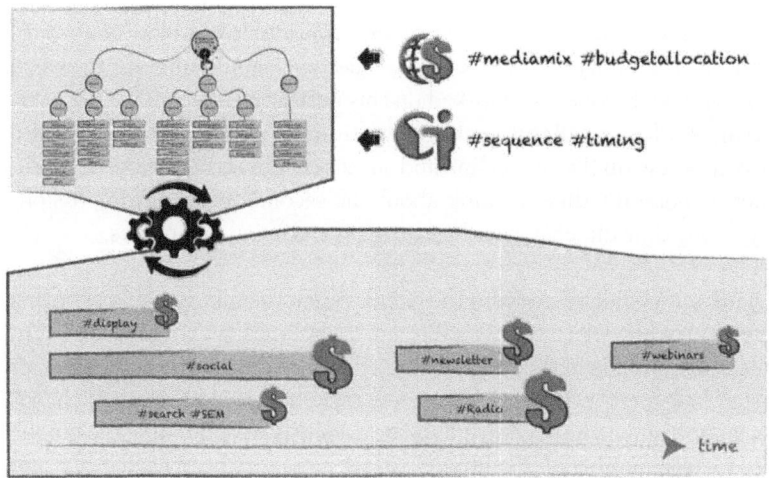

In the real marketing world, this means we have avoided the last touch attribution and change to a more sophisticated attribution model, where all interactions are included in the predictive model. This is a discipline that most of my clients struggled with, because aside from the pure analytics, the organization of the paid, owned, earned activation layer is an extremely complex transformation project.

Demand Windows

Before I begin, I'd like to highlight the importance of this topic. We analyzed our lab purely from the owner of the houses and the striker, dinos, and artists. Now let's bring in the people visiting our houses because they aren't mechanical systems designed to catch the balls, though just in case, we use the best working mix or sequence of techniques.

Also, we have a high time dependency, since some of them are more likely to catch a ball in the morning when they are fresh and fit, instead of when they're tired in the afternoon; others (the sporty ones) may be more motivated to catch balls as part of their after-work training program, or some may only catch balls if they're in the back of the room, or in the front of the room — thus our easy segmentation of front and back no longer works, as soon as people start walking around our houses.

Since we analyzed their behavior and added attributes to their cookie ID earlier too, we should use our central data lake to figure out the time and location-dependent analytics. We should use the conversion rate of caught balls to find out the best demand window. Our analytics model has to predict the timeframe and location that our target audience is most willing to catch a ball. This means we're enhancing the attributes like "music lover" based on our proven hypothesis that "the likelihood of music lovers to catch balls in the morning in front of the room is x times higher than average." Now we can store the data like this: "music lover," "demand window to catch balls 8–11:00 am, front, likelihood 3x."

It's honestly as simple as that. Though it may sound like a small topic when it's described like this, in the real marketing world, this is the masterpiece in data-driven marketing. Why? This is the ultimate combination of campaign, audience, and success data in one single predictive model.

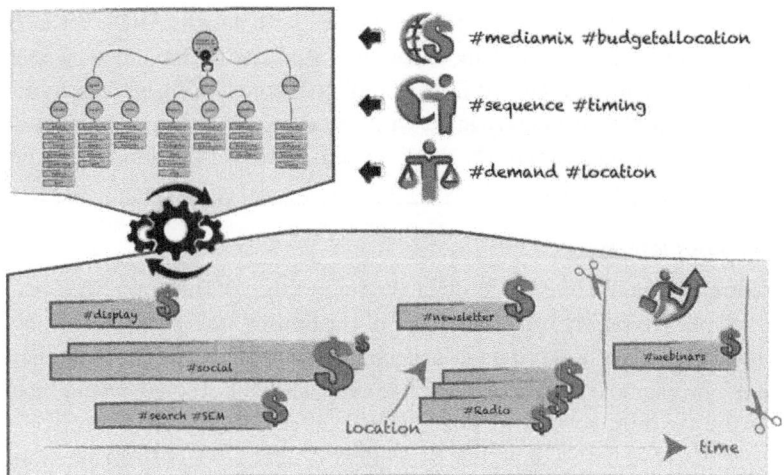

Since this book is about data-driven marketing, I'd like to remind you that this only works if our data management and customer data platform is filled with all the information, locations, and timestamps on the lowest level — the single interaction with a person out of our target audience, including timestamps — and this is to be used for all striker techniques. A question I'm always asking in my marketing transformation projects is: *are you able to tell me the number of impressions and actions per unique user, timestamp, location, and activation channel?* If not, there's room for improvement regarding your data-driven marketing maturity.

For me, another interesting fact we should focus on is: we haven't increased the number of measures by a significant number (only timestamp and location) with all the enhancement to our lab. We've just added a lot of new dimensions and processes!

Process and Rules	Organization
• Media Mix Optimization • Multi-touch Attribution Modelling	• Channel Manager and Specialists • Data Scientists
Platforms	Data and Dimension
• Activation Platforms • Next best action frameworks	• Media Channel and Activation Type • Timestamps • Location

Multiple actions — goals, funnels and customer journeys

After the chapter about channel mix, attribution, and demand windows, I'd like to open the next domain. Let's add more complexity to our lab by introducing another type of time dependency. As always, the customer should be the focus of every new enhancement.

To recap: we started by increasing our throwing team to paid, owned, and earned strikers; all of them should be using a broad set of different throwing techniques. We also analyzed the most successful sequence of throwing techniques depending on the demand windows of our target audience.

Marketing Funnels

To be honest, the entire time that we focused on the goal of "catching a ball" — there was only one dedicated action we had in mind and that all our optimization run against. But what if we introduce here a sequence of goals similar to our attribution models too? This would mean that we don't rely on one single goal, instead, we define a funnel of action steps where we like to "push" our target audience through.

Within our lab this might be a stack of the following goals:

- Generate awareness that there are balls in the air
- Let them catch one for the first time and give them the time to look at it
- Put pressure on the ones who like the balls and motivate them to get more
- A clear call to action to buy a basket to put all the balls in
- Give them the possibility to share their emotions to earn some viral network effects
- A clear call to action to buy a towel to put on top of the basket
- Remind them months later about their positive emotions during the first run and sell a new enhancement in the form of a corresponding lid instead of the towel.

We're able to leverage the full set of analytics we used for media-mix, attribution modeling, and demand windows to optimize each step in our series of goals above. The conversion rate from our initial step to the next ones and the direct one from step n to n+1 gives us a good way to stay on top of our complete funnel. By adding the costs that we invested in each layer, we are getting a KPI for the cost per actions (CPA) — once for the full funnel and once for each dedicated goal.

Taking into consideration that the different conversions are caused by different strikers (paid, owned, and earned) within different houses (campaigns) and different throwing techniques and balls (channels and branded content) we end up with a full-fledged PEO dashboard.

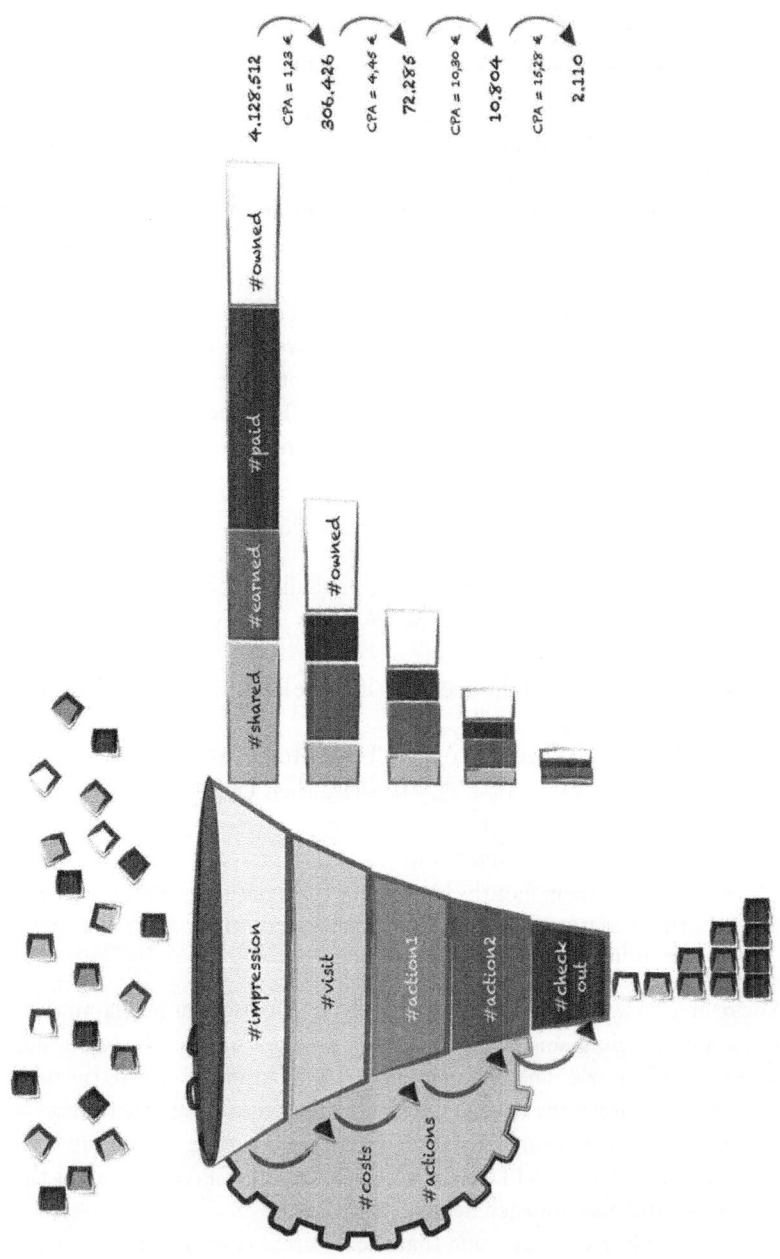

Customer Journeys

Let's keep this experiment up and think about the matching lab versus reality. Do we have just one single path through our funnel? It means all the people are going to run in the same direction step by step through the funnel. This isn't realistic, but it helps in tailoring our actions to the needs of our customers, but there are ways to further push the likelihood for conversion by introducing the concepts of journeys.

We can anticipate that in the real world, there will be visitors to our houses who directly run to one of the corners to buy a basket as they have a high need for it, which looks like there's no need for any awareness balls upfront. However, others we've carefully driven from awareness, through interest towards an intent for buying, but then they may get influenced by someone else we weren't able to control (e.g. an influencer). This means these people get pushed back to awareness or may fall totally out of our strategic audience, and tactical segments.

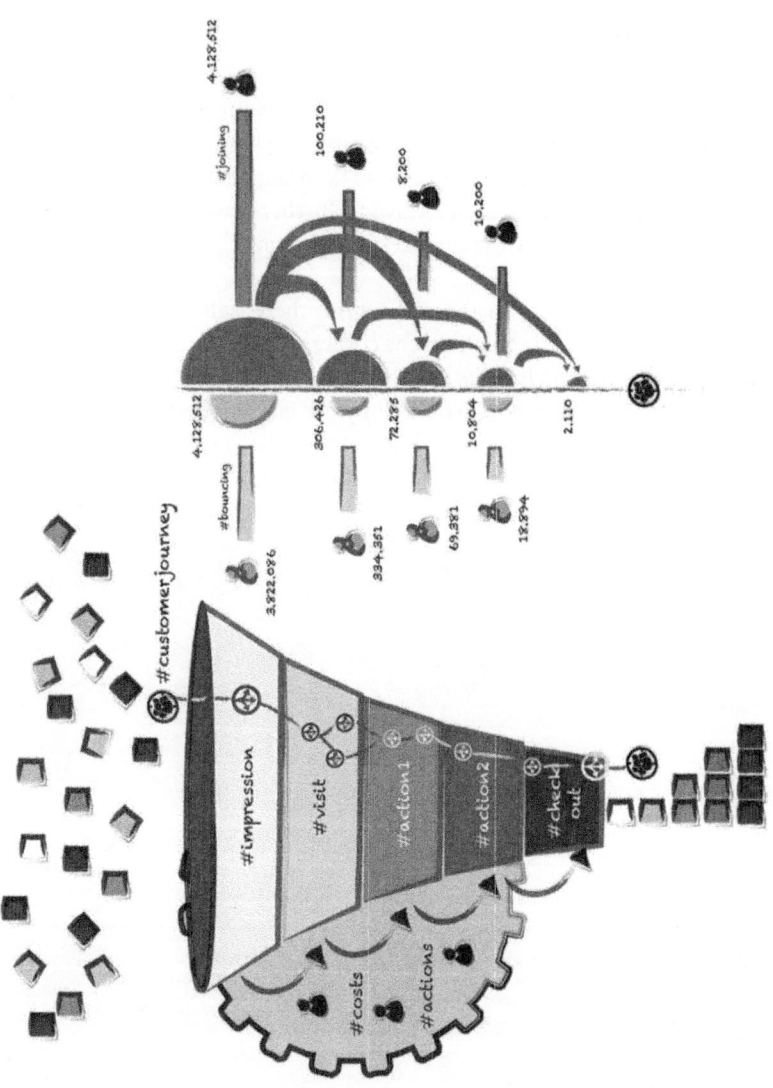

A customer journey tries to optimize these different target segments with the best fit we can imagine. This can be done by going beyond the pure funnel and defining short stints within the funnel from one layer to the next, or even beyond several layers in one journey.

Optimizing the different journeys instead of using the complete funnel allows us to serve customer needs on a higher level. The result is an increased aggregated total conversion rate towards the lowest level of our complete funnel.

Our tiny lab of throwing some balls at people in a room evolved to a high-performing PEO marketing machine that allows us to define a set of goals in a funnel, and execute this time-dependent against our hyper accurately segmented target audiences within customer journeys.

Process and Rules	Organization
• Funnel Management • Customer Journey Management	• Funnel/Journey Manager and **Specialists**
Platforms	Data and Dimension
• Customer Journey Management Platforms • Realtime Customer Journey Analytics	• Goals • Funnels and Funnel Layer • Customer Journey

With the advent of new marketing clouds, we're able to steer away from this push mode by training our strikers on the best sequence of techniques within journeys as the only way to get in contact with our target audience. Let's see what this means.

Mat Robo — trigger-based campaign automation

Let's add a fourth player to our team, I'd like to give him the name "Mat Robo", but there's one twist — he's not human. It's a ball-throwing machine that reacts within sub-seconds on every single interaction with one of our customers. Thus, whenever someone has caught a red ball, Mat automatically waits for 5 minutes and then throws a second green ball towards them. Nobody has to be trained from our current paid, owned, and earned strikers to perfect shots with the best fitting location and time. Plus, Mat is incredibly intelligent; depending on whether the customer has taken the second one Mat will wait for a further 10 minutes to throw a third yellow ball. Or if he's taken the green one, this one directly asks him to buy a basket for his balls. The nice benefit of this new player is that he doesn't have a salary. The trade-off is the high initial investment to buy him and put him in place, as well as the ongoing maintenance of the mechanics and the software operating system.

Campaign Automation

If we take a closer look at Mat Robo, it will help us to understand the power of automated support for our existing team. The inner core is a processor combined with an intelligent piece of software. This allows us to define trigger-based interactions with our preferred target audiences. The system is connected via high-speed lines to our central data lake, which will be able to constantly check who has interacted within which house.

Modern Mat Robo systems don't rely only on manual triggers someone installed at the beginning as a starting point into their configuration. The Mat Robo system includes a component that automatically optimizes the throwing tactics, the sequence of balls, and all other customer interactions supported by the power of artificially generated insights and predictions in real-time. Journeys can now include triage of actions, waiting positions, or similar actions at one point in time.

Last but not least, the automated system is fully connected to a mechanic interaction system, that allows it to throw balls towards our target audiences. While the early versions of Mat Robo only allowed one or two throwing techniques, the current state-of-the-art platforms can execute copies of all techniques used in our paid, owned striker teams. Mat Robo is more of an automated copy of the paid and owned strikers instead of the fourth striker beside the existing PEO ones.

Trigger Based Campaigns

The machine can go beyond this push of balls by providing fully new techniques that are similar, but more advanced to our owned ones. Instead of actively seeking for the target audience and throwing balls towards them, we use Mat Robo to set up a pull-based ecosystem. This means the automated system allows them to provide balls, baskets, and surrounding information about them in a way that the target audience can decide on their own if, where, and when they like to get one of them. We are going away from the pure push within our paid campaign-driven approach and towards a combination of pull/push interactions. Again, putting the customer journey first in our marketing approach will help to serve our customers in the most convenient way for them, and successful way for us. Welcome to the complex world of intelligent data-driven marketing.

This automation of marketing actions again adds a large layer of complexity to our lab. As this is a machine combining software, hardware, and mechanic components, we require different technicians who can maintain and configure Mat Robo, as well as an organization knowing how to run such a robot. We need an overview of the actions we've activated; in the real world, we often end-up in hundreds of different customer interactions and journeys we configured, sometimes overlapping or trying to optimize against different goals that are no longer in our focus.

Process and Rules	Organization
• Marketing Automation • Trigger-Based Campaign Management	• Marketing Automation Manager and Specialist
Platforms	Data and Dimension
• Automated Campaign Execution Platforms (Marketing Clouds) • AI-based interactions centers, including push journey actions	• Triggers

Getting served in such a way by us may cause our clients to become stressed, so much so that they start behaving differently than we originally expected and the initial data has shown us.

I'd like to hurry on with my amendments to the lab with some words about annoyed users and the necessity of frequency caps and automation maintenance, and governance.

My bag is full — frequency caps and campaign maintenance

There's a famous slogan that goes like this: "emotions are the new currency of data-driven customer experience." What does this mean exactly? With all the data we collect, the highly sophisticated predictive models we developed, and the perfect agile campaign execution and automation, in the end, it's the customer themselves who decide what their next preferred action is. In most cases, they're heavily guided by their own emotions, and not by the rational logic of attribution models and time dependencies. Intelligent data-driven marketing should consider this and has to put the customer themselves in the middle of every analysis and action. The focus changes from the context of finding the best placement for activation (e.g. advertisement, message, appointment, etc.) to a full audience-driven and customer-centric way of working.

Frequency capping

This takes us to the management of frequency caps. I guess the majority of readers may already be aware of its importance. Avoiding having too much contact in the form of push activations and pulled customer interactions to hopefully not annoy the customer is one of the most challenging tasks in our modern marketing world.

In our lab, this means at a certain point in time, parts of our audience are no longer willing to catch a ball or buy further bags. Their behavior changes suddenly, and they are no longer showing the reactions we predicted several times before. Or it's more likely that they won't show a reaction, even if we throw another thousand balls towards them or allow them to pick up one by themselves.

The good thing, all the data we collect helps us to find the perfect frequency cap. There are two things we have to consider though: the first is the non-efficient conversion from people who are beyond this perfect cap. We should spend more effort on these people who have been involved in one of our previous actions, instead equally throwing balls towards all of them.

Secondly, we should take care that nobody is involved in any activations above our perfect frequency cap as this is lost money and will annoy our customers.

We predicted this perfect amount of thrown balls for the maximum of conversion, everything above has no longer any significant effect on conversion and shapes the behavior of our target audience.

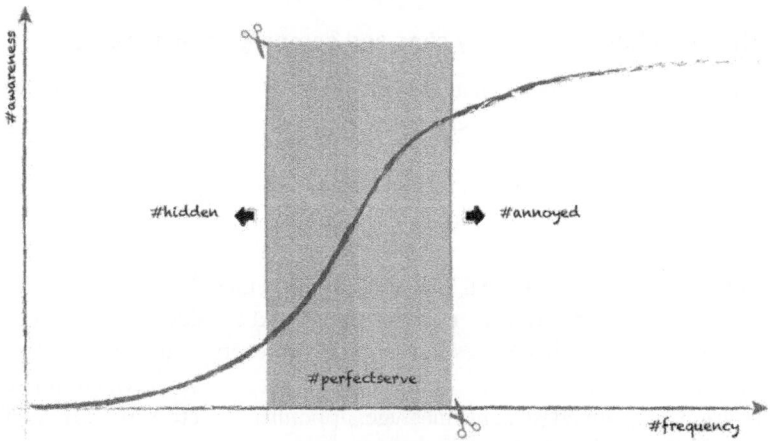

So, if we agree on the shown curve and perfect efficiency at the frequency cap, we need to take care to act in both directions. This has further implications that need to be considered in our lab.

The first is the need to enhance our lab environment or also take care that the reality is often a bit more complex than playing around with thoughts and imaginary experiments. We just postulated that our central data management and customer data platform is connected to all strikers, even if they're humans or machines. On top, we have our target audience that can easily be identified by just placing the cookie in their pockets.

Cross-device and cross-platform

We need to do another short stray from the main topic and steer away from our idealistic lab environment. I have more than 22 years' consulting experience with big enterprises in the field of CRM, sales, and marketing. For this reason, I know the Gedankenexperiment works quite well to illustrate most of the issues that need to be overcome in an intelligent data-driven marketing setup. But the cross-device and cross-system topic is not part of this lab. What's behind these two "cross" topics? Read on and find out.

Cross-device deals with the fact that we don't directly reach our target audience with a ball normally. Instead, we reach their devices in the form of smartphones, desktop computers, or any other internet-protocol-based devices (TV box, voice bots, etc.). In our lab, a baseball may simulate the gloves our people are wearing; the cookie is placed within the glove and not the person's pocket, which means all gloves people are wearing have different unique IDs.

To run our perfect customer journey and campaign, we have to combine these different devices owned by members of our target audience in our data management and customer data platform to a joined customer profile. This can be done through statistics, e.g. we just measure how often we've seen the same set of devices in a wireless network at the same time. The more robust solution is to rely on a login name that has to be used whenever we're in contact with our target audience. This is widely used in social networks like Facebook and explains how powerful they are in the eco-system of marketing. A login also allows the vice-versa insight — when different members of our target audience use one device.

Cross-Platform is more of an internal challenge. Within our central office, the data-lake and the houses where we get to contact our target audience are a bit too simplistic. In the real world, we are far away from one platform for storing all of these contact points. Often, we're not even able to get the full set of data; we have lots of "wallet gardens" in the marketing universe.

Normally, we see a conglomerate of platforms and systems that are used to serve the customers (pull) and actively reach them (push). All these platforms use cookies, mobile IDs, etc. to identify and tag their customers. To implement working frequency caps, it's necessary to implement a data management and customer data platform that can sync all these IDs within one single profile to give us the full overview of all interactions in one place. It would be some kind of 360-degree view on one prospect or customer.

We assumed that we have a perfect data-lake in the middle of our cities that allows us to capture and re-use all customer interactions. But what if we have some "wallet gardens" in some of our houses that don't allow them to capture information about touchpoints or if our data-lake is split into several silos — each containing information for one or two striker and techniques. This is how our reality looks like; most social networks and video platforms don't allow us to collect user-specific information. The most effective networks often just rely on the principle "give me money and I do something great for you" without giving the advertiser a full insight into the people they reached. Instead, they show impressive cost per actions and conversion rates, all context-centric and far away from real audience-centric events on the lowest level. It means if we'd like to run cross-system frequency caps, we need to overcome most of the barriers in the marketing ecosystem and should keep in mind that there are wallet gardens out there, that don't allow us to reach this goal one hundred percent.

Real-Time & Negative Segments
The second enhancement to our lab is to drill deeper into the psychology behind awareness and performance campaigns, including the pulled customer interactions for tailored customer journeys. The frequency cap needs to take care of certain exceptions or master triggers to stop any execution once the final goal is reached. What do I mean by this? Well, we all know the annoying pattern: we buy something in our preferred online shop and for days after, we're pursued by ads that promote "our bought product" exactly or at the very at least, similar things? I'm sure no advertiser in the world is willing to send these ads and spend additional money on these customers — but hey, they've reached the final funnel layer!

The problem is our cross-device, system frequency cap, and the ability to take care of master triggers to stop the execution. Upon the first examination, this appears to be a problem easily solved by stopping activations towards the people involved in one of our desired actions gets more and more complex the more we dig into the details. We need to work in real-time and with "negative segments" to actively exclude people in our campaigns. Using the pattern of collecting data, building target audiences, finding the best fitting promotions and products to run a campaign exactly leads to this effect, it even amplifies it.

Normally the target audiences are transferred to the activation layer in the form of cookie IDs, mobile IDs, or even email addresses and phone numbers regularly, and not in real-time. The campaign starts and our strikers move forward by throwing balls towards the target audiences until a) the money is off, b) the campaign end-date is reached or c) the guy we like to hit has reached his frequency cap. But what about all the people who engaged with the desired action (caught a ball and bought a basket) before we reached the budget, end-date or frequency cap or final funnel layer? Our tactic from above is to spend more money and to push them to the perfect number of ads to maximize the conversion rate!

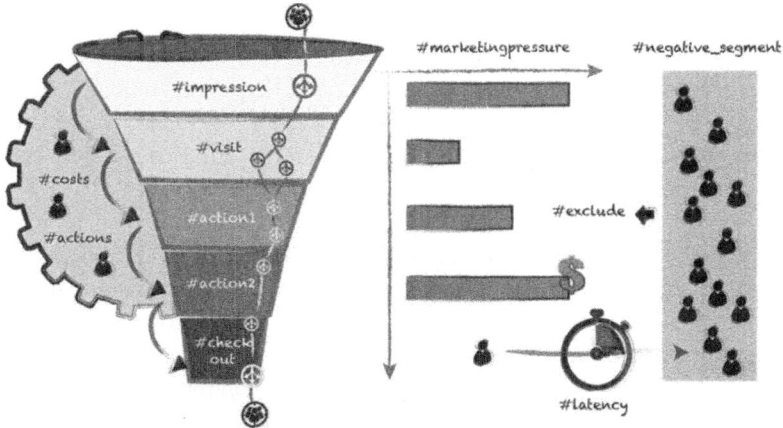

To avoid this pitfall, we have to sync (more or less) all the people who engaged in real-time (e.g. bought the product, downloaded the video, et.) in a segment that we exclude in each throw. It means all media channels and all activation platforms are "always on" and connected to our data management and customer data platform. We sync this negative segment in real-time to all our activation channels and partners. You can imagine this isn't an easy thing to do, and in 22 years, I've only seen a hand full of advertisers who have mastered this successfully.

Process and Rules	Organization
• Cross-Device Management • Cross-System Identification • Frequency capping • Realtime Audience Management (negative segments)	• IT Experts for the marketing technology stack
Platforms	Data and Dimension
• Customer 360 — Profile Platform	• Frequency Cap • Exception Triggers

The Perpetuum mobile — sharing, communities, and influencing

So far, we have only talked about the interaction of our target audience with one of our strikers or Mat Robo, who served the best fitting information or products to them. But what about the interaction between all of them within one of our houses, or even within the city?

Viral Sharing

Due to the advent of smart devices and the fact that in our modern world everything can be shared, we should take advantage of an effect called "viral sharing." Let's try to build up some kind of Perpetuum mobile, which means we invest a certain amount of energy (in our case money and owned effort), and from that moment in time, the system runs forever with the same or higher velocity. But is this a dream or plausible reality?

If we play it the right way, and with some positive network effects, it could be a reality. Instead of convincing our audience with a massive number of pitches with different balls, we have to focus more on some kind of creative flight-objects. We may use some cubicles that show super creative images or even a cool video but on each side. On top, we're putting a few hidden calls to actions in the video or just show our brand to generate awareness. We now throw them on the target audience, or Mat Robo tries to identify the most effective interaction to serve the new object. What we would like to reach is a viral effect. Instead of reaching our frequency cap in a perfect attribution sequence and journey, one or two just grab the cube and start talking with their neighbors about it. The tiny button on it automatically generates a short video hologram in front of all their friends. In some cases, when creativity, initial push, and a bit of good luck comes together, we will be able to generate a viral positive network effect. People who might see the video hologram might start liking it or retweeting it with other "friends." And at one point in time, there's no need to throw further cubes into the audience. The message will be spread massively around the network of people visiting our houses. These are impressions for free as every like, retweet, or share we see in the network is one more who gets aware of our brand or who might interact based on our call to action.

The production costs are much higher for the cube, but the number of shared impressions we may generate and the conversions we see that lead to a cost per action that's far below the ones we see on pure paid throwing techniques.

And on top of this, it's a new challenge for the guy sitting in front of the whiteboard and reporting on what happens in the houses. Up until now, the only tracking we did was who's involved in the paid, owned, and earned ways of reaching the target audience. So, we need to measure the number of additional actions (e.g. impressions, clicks) caused by the likes, retweets, and shares in the social network of our audience as well.

As this is possible for all actions, regardless of whether they're paid, owned or earned, we then introduce a new dimension called "shared" on top of all three. Welcome to the world of PESO dashboards in data-driven marketing!

The Net Promotor Score — measure happiness

I'd like to introduce a new KPI called "net promoter score," that gives us some kind of level about the willingness of our reached audience to share the brand experience within their network.

This is one of the most discussed KPIs in intelligent data-driven marketing. From my point of view, it's the only one we can measure in our lab, as well as the real world. I've seen a lot of people telling me this KPI doesn't make any sense, but not one of them could give me a better alternative to it.

The calculation is based on the easy question "on a scale of 1 to 10, how likely you are to share the brand experience within your (social) network?" We then subtract the percent of ratings of 1–6 from the 9–10, then we get a new KPI — the "net promoter score."

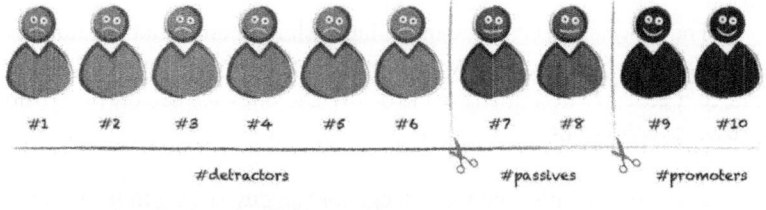

Let's say a few more lines on this topic of viral effects without massive activation budget, but higher production costs, before we finish. We can enhance the willingness to catch balls and buy baskets by influencing the audience in various other ways.

Influencer

First, we could take advantage of a few heroes within our audience. Some of them are known as celebrities, good sportsmen, singers, etc. Why not use them to influence the audience in the way we acted above? Instead of using the budget to buy balls, we give it to them and ask them to show how they catch balls, how they use our baskets, etc. The effect is similar, but people will be more likely to buy them. And as everything can be shared, the chances to become viral is also here.

Especially with the advent of social networks, we can contract people with a high number of friends (followers) in the target audience. We could pay them to speak about our baskets in their "normal and natural" conversations within their network. These influencers are very effective and help to generate similar to what our sponsored people from above were doing; generating awareness of our brand and the willingness to follow one of our preferred call to actions.

Communities

Secondly, we follow the paid, owned, and earned paradigm again in this section. While influencers are mostly paid, we can build up communities by placing nice chairs, tables, and coffee machines in one of the free corners of our houses. This motivates people to sit down and drink a warm cup of coffee, which will lead to them sharing their personal experiences they've had with balls, baskets, and the eco-system surrounding them.

Guerilla teams and experiential marketing

A third way to gain awareness is to be a bit more creative by just sponsoring a few selected people from the audience, contract the influencers, or build communities. Instead, we put "hidden players" into the game. They start introducing our baskets in many creative ways to the audience.

There are many ways of influencing the audience including use the budget to run events within the city or in one of our houses. As an example, we can get our 'owned' people interacting with the target audience and they'll do things like organizing an event called "the ball catching challenge," or they'll give out baseball gloves for free. These will help to motivate more people to catch our balls or buy a basket to put them in. The intention is that they show our brand, products, and call to actions in a subtle way. It makes a huge difference to the customers because they're getting a friendlier experience than they did before, with just the balls being thrown.

A real-life example would be instead of spending money on TV ads, an advertiser started to organize a Europe-wide street soccer tournament with events happening in the inner cities. It included surrounding music stations, drinks, and beach areas for people to watch how others play the game. The consumer activation team sampled the new product and the full area was branded by the advertiser's logo and colors. Finally, free vouchers for discounts helped to sell the new product and link the tournament activities and investment towards the additional sales.

There's no limit on how we interact with our preferred audience; the creativity is back and gives us the possibility to differentiate the way we access the market. What should be clear here, is that we need our tiny gatekeeper dinos to collect as much information as possible on the lowest level of single customer interaction.

Process and Rules	Organization
• Viral Sharing	• Social Manage and Specialists
• Influencer Marketing	• Influencer Manager and Specialists
• Community Management	• Community Manager
• Guerilla and Experiential Marketing	• Guerilla Teams
Platforms	Data and Dimension
• Community Management Platforms	• Shared (on top of paid, owned, and earned)
• Event Management and Planning	
• Influencer Management Portals	• Net Promoter Score

Summary — Gedankenexperiment 2.0

So let's summarize all the complex information we've put together step by step and place it into our elementary virtual lab 1.0 in one comprehensive bullet list. This gives us a good overview of how a data-driven marketing machine should look like:

Process and Rules	Organization
• Strategic marketing planning [Marketing Resource Management] • Interconnected homes [Campaign and Media Planning] • Creative Management [Content Management] • Dynamic Creative Optimization and branded content • 70-20-10 Rule • Agile Marketing • Hyper Accurate Targeting • Frequency Management • Look-a-like Modelling • Programmatic Marketing • Data Protection Management • Marketing Partner Management • Cost Planning and Management Media Mix Optimization • Multi-touch Attribution Modelling • Funnel Management • Customer Journey Management • Marketing Automation • Trigger Based Campaign Management • Cross-Device Management • Cross-System Identification • Frequency capping • Realtime Audience Management (negative segments) • Viral Sharing • Influencer Marketing • Community Management • Guerilla and Experiential Marketing	• The striker who throws the balls • Data Analyst who fills the whiteboard • Central Data Team who handles the different data requests • Sprint teams • Creative Production and Delivery • Data Protection Manager • Audience Specialist • Programmatic Specialist • Channel Manager and Specialists • Data Scientists • Funnel/Journey Manager and Specialists • Marketing Automation Manager and Specialist • IT Experts for the marketing technology stack • Social Manage and Specialists • Influencer Manager and Specialists • Community Manager • Guerilla Teams

Platforms	Data and Dimension
• Central lake of Audience Profiles/ [DMP and CDP] • Campaign planning, preparation and controlling system [marketing resource management within a marketing cloud] • The gatekeeper dinos [tag management system] • Personalization and A/B testing engine • Digital Asset Management to deliver and store content [DAM] • Data Sharing Platforms for 2nd and 3rd party data • Predictive Data Management and Customer Data Enhancements and Frameworks • Distributed Marketing Planning Platform • Finance and Controlling Platform • Activation Platforms • Next best action frameworks • Customer Journey Management Platforms • Realtime Customer Journey Analytics • Automated Campaign Execution Platforms (Marketing Clouds) • AI-based interaction centers, incl. push journey actions • Customer 360 — Profile Platform • Community Management Platforms • Event Management and Planning • Influencer Management Portals	• The name of the Cities, Regions & Countries → marketing programs, plans, and brands. • Colors and Forms • Sprints • Type of investment (known, new, innovative) • Consent Status • With the connection to 2nd and 3rd party data market, the amount of dimension we now can use is depending on the data-sharing platform we use, and what they can provide. As said above, 20 to 30 thousand attributes per cookie can be bought on the current data sharing market. • Paid, owned and earned classifications • Different Cost layers • Media Channel and Activation Type • Timestamps • Location • Goals • Funnels and Funnel Layer • Customer Journey • Triggers • Frequency Cap • Exception Triggers • Shared (on top of paid, owned and earned) • Net Promoter Score

It should be obvious, after all this, that holistic and intelligent data-driven marketing is not an easy job! While on the one hand, all the topics above have to be considered within your transformation and implementation efforts, as well as the ongoing change and target operating model, needs to be installed (enablement program).

For that reason, I'd like to close the virtual lab 2.0 and hurry on to use some fundamental physical principals and copy them over into the marketing universe. This will show you how to be data-driven in this new world and what kind of pitfalls you will face, as this is predictable by natural laws.

Using more physics on marketing

Stepping away from virtual labs, now we'll turn back to the inner core and idea of this book: using physical theorems and algorithms in the world of marketing!

The starting point will be the closed-loop marketing I've used within my examples above; this includes the continuous flow of strategic marketing planning, campaign execution and automation, and insight generation based on a perfectly orchestrated technology stack.

We will then see how these dynamic systems come to equilibrium and how to move a system of reference to a higher velocity by eliminating waste through the use of lean principals. This also counts for every change program and the way we "enable" our organization to follow us on the journey towards intelligent data-driven marketing.

The 2nd law of thermodynamics will teach us about the efforts needed to transform a marketing organization to be data-driven first and foremost. It will also highlight the need for a continuous flow of change.

Together with the theory of solid-state-physics and how complex systems are built, these two chapters will provide all you need to start a business transformation towards the world of intelligent data-driven marketing.

Finally, I'll end this chapter with Einstein. I support every reader expects to find him in a book about physics, however, I like using his relativity theory to show the impact of creativity within marketing. All the discussions about data and audiences pushed this topic a bit outside of the focus of new CMOs.

Let us change this and bring back the essentials: all is relative to the creativity of your customer activation.

Fluid dynamics — "reaching the perfect flow"

The physics behind — the law of continuity

The volume of fluid moving through the pipe at any local point can be quantified in terms of the volume flow rate, which is equal to the area of the pipe (A_i) at the point I multiplied by the velocity of the fluid (v_i). The volume flow rate must be constant throughout the whole pipe. You can write the equation of continuity for fluids like this:

$$A_1 * v_1 = A_2 * v_2$$

The equation says that whenever the cross-section of the pipe gets smaller, the velocity of the fluid increases, and vice-versa — in the case of the cross-section getting larger, the fluid velocity decreases.

We all know this phenomenon when we're going out into the backyard to water our plants. To reach the one directly in front of us we just use the hosepipe like it is. But to reach the flowers far in the back of the yard, we place our thumb on top of the pipe, this narrows down the area the water flows through. The effect is that we apply more pressure and therefore the water jet running through has a much higher velocity.

What does this mean for marketing — reaching the perfect flow

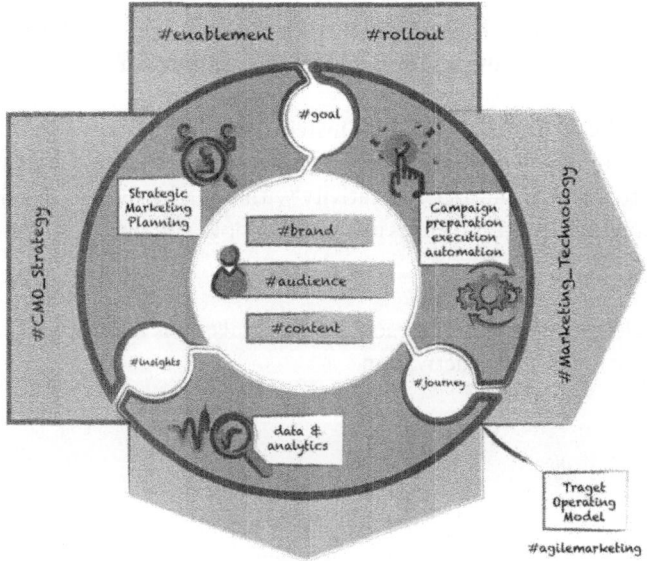

Looking back to our Gedankenexperiment, we could argue that this is quite static. It just describes (even in its most sophisticated 2.0 version) the single execution of some marketing programs and highlights the most important topics and tasks.

But a normal marketing department built with communications teams, brand teams, guerrilla and field-force teams, event and sponsorship, IT, etc. is a complex setup that needs to work perfectly together.

Returning to the fluid dynamics of different teams, processes, and IT platforms, it can be seen as a closed loop of different pipe pieces, put together with different joints, switches, velocity meters, and valves. The running campaign itself is the fluid pressed through this pipeline.

Now let's assume what will happen if we've orchestrated a perfect strategic marketing planning. We plan for several programs containing multiple campaigns and channel activations, and the underlying IT system is directly connected to our general ledger and yearly financial planning cycle. All our approved programs get automatically funded, but the joints towards our creative management process and also the switch to the multiple agencies aren't designed properly. It means we see a bottleneck in the flow to deliver the demand of new creatives in time for each running campaign, and also the local teams and media agencies can't push out the number of planned activations. The term 'bottleneck' means squeezing the cross-section of our pipeline. The natural effect of the law of continuity predicts that the organization and platforms behind it need to work faster. So, they have to increase their velocity.

In the real marketing world, this causes stress on the teams because they need to deliver what's expected of them. We would end up with poor quality, roughly executed campaigns.

So, if we'd like to build the perfect marketing machine, we need to analyze the flow of campaigns through this pipeline out of strategic marketing planning, campaign execution and automation, and insight generation. If we look at this diversified technology stack, then we see that only perfectly orchestrated IT platforms avoid the pitfalls of building bottlenecks within our execution.

The final result is a high-performing marketing machine, that is fed by budget, data, and creativity, and has an outcome of a seamlessly delivered global portfolio of all paid, owned, and earned activations.

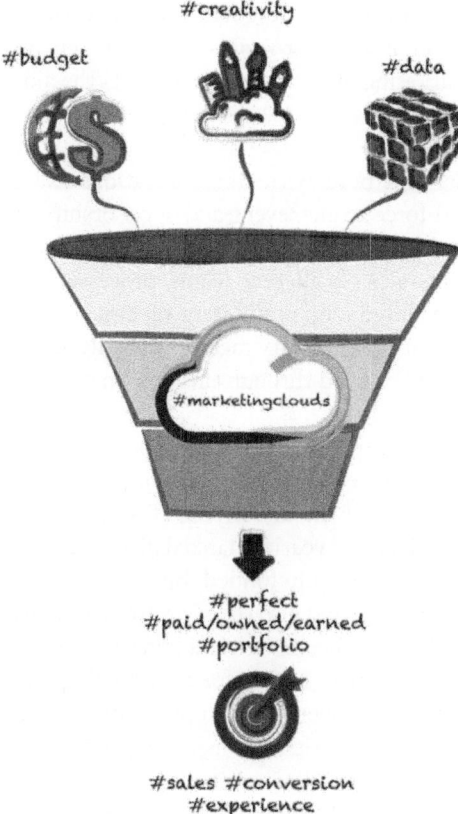

This is similar to the Kanban and Lean approach of production and supply chain processes. The main goal is to eliminate the maximum amount of waste and implement a lean flow of production. Kanban guarantees that in case I need a special screw and tool to fix a piece at a machine both are there, just one arm's length away. The box of screws will never be empty but it doesn't have too many pieces.

This physical algorithm brings the dynamic into our initial system of reference. Within our transformation program, as we head towards intelligent data-driven marketing set up, we need to carefully analyze the flow from the early ideation that we'd like to do. This would be done by planning towards the execution plus automation, down to the final measurement of success data. Whenever we find a few bottlenecks, we should think about a possible solution to overcome this issue. We will then add the solution to our transformation backlog in a continuous wind of change.

Harmonic oscillation — "everything is in motion"

The physics behind — the law of mechanics

A long time ago, within physics, Isaac Newton defined, "action equals reaction." Therefore, with every change we introduced to our system of reference, we'll see a counteraction often pushing us back to the point that we started at. The result is an ongoing back and forth until we reach a new equilibrium; such a system and behavior is described as a damped harmonic oscillation.

In classical mechanics, a harmonic oscillator is a system that, when displaced from its equilibrium position, experiences a restoring force, ($F = m * \ddot{x}$) proportional to the displacement (x).

$$\ddot{x} + a\dot{x} + bx = c$$

If F is the only force acting on the system, then it's called a simple harmonic oscillator. In the case of frictional force (damping: $a * \dot{x}$) proportional to the velocity is also present, the harmonic oscillator is described as a damped oscillator.

Then, if an external time-dependent force is present, the harmonic oscillator is described as a driven oscillator.

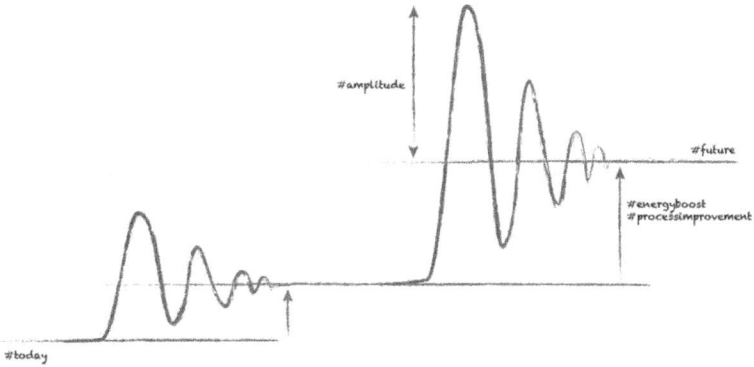

We also know this phenomenon in the form of a nice mechanic system with a few balls in a row. If we lift the first (which does nothing else than add energy) the system starts running like a pendulum —from left to right, and back. The friction between the balls, robes, air, etc. is a counteracting force that brings the system down to its initial state. If we bring in ongoing energy, the system never stops, and, depending on the power, the balls will reach a dedicated amplitude.

What does this mean for marketing — everything is in motion

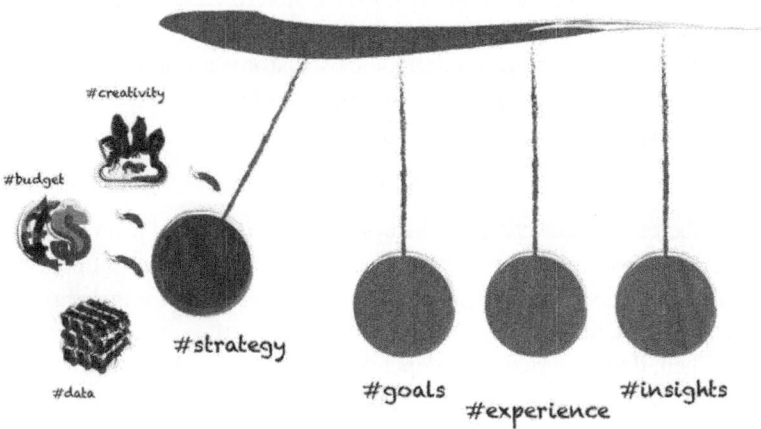

As the law of dynamics has shown us what happens whenever we start designing and running a closed-loop process for data-driven marketing, the harmonic oscillation is teaching us how to change systems. This can be the improvement process of executing campaigns and user journeys, but also the change within an organization.

As soon as we bring in an impulse in the form of new additional energy into the mechanic system, it starts running over the later equilibrium and level. Like a pendulum, the system needs some time to stabilize at its new baseline. The additional energy, in this case, is similar to process improvement, organizational change, or system update that we introduce to our marketing ecosystem. So, don't expect things would get better straight away, and certainly don't believe in the initial improvements — they will fall back after the first enthusiasm has gone, or the complexity starts raining again. Then you should start measuring the velocity of your marketing organization and monitor the KPI carefully with a trend chart.

The same happens if we start looking at the direct flow of our perfect closed-loop campaign planning, preparation, execution, and automation towards the final analytics and insights set up. The optimization we will find in our ongoing A/B testing may show massive effects at first, but later it will drop down below the final level — just like the pendulum. This means a single snapshot of measures and KPIs won't reveal the truth to us. Instead, we need to rely on trend charts to see how the measures will evolve.

To win the intelligent data-driven marketing world, you need to be successful in all the programs and campaigns that you're running on a long-term basis. A single increase of your click-through-rate or fantastic email open rates are far away from continuously increased velocity and sustainable success of your marketing activations.

The law of thermodynamics — "flow of change"

The physics behind — The second law of thermodynamics

Entropy (S) is a measure of disorder within a macroscopic system. The second law of thermodynamics states that the total entropy can't decrease over time for an isolated system of reference, that is, a system in which neither energy nor matter can enter or leave.

$$\Delta S \geq 0$$

The total entropy can remain constant in ideal cases where the system is in a steady-state (equilibrium) or is undergoing a reversible process. In all other real cases, the total entropy always increases, and the process is irreversible. The increase in entropy accounts for the irreversibility of natural processes, and the asymmetry between the future and the past. Or this could happen the other way round and it's not as complicated; it takes energy to order a system, and disorder will evolve automatically.

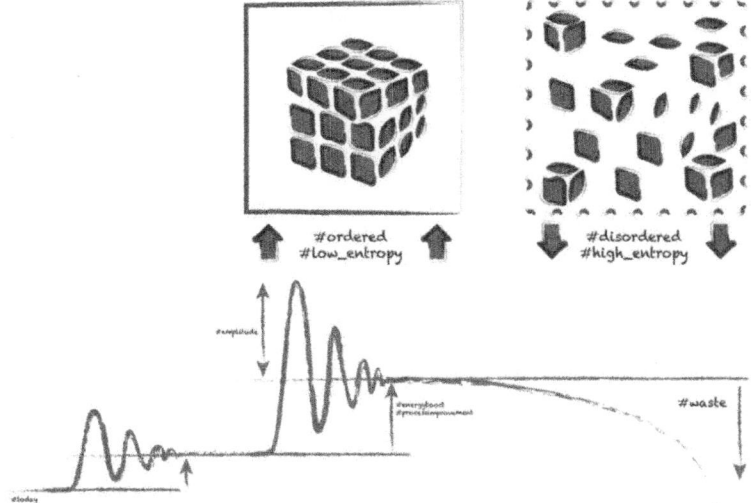

I think all of us who have young kids at home know about this phenomenon. It takes mom and dad a lot of energy every night to get rid of the chaos these young hurricanes are producing — and they can produce this hectic atmosphere within seconds. And, to be honest, I'm still waiting (and have been for the last 10 years) for the kid's rooms to show some kind of order without invested energy on dad's end.

What does this mean for marketing — continuous flow of change

With more than 23 years of experience with transformations and business consulting, I'm deeply convinced that this second law can also be applied within every enterprise to all running processes, organizations, IT platforms, and data taxonomies.

It's clear that without a constant flow of energy in the form of controlled change, enablement, and incremental improvements that are of a wonderfully designed new maturity level, will just erode over time. For a very long time, this was a more than profitable business model for strategy consulting — design new blueprints, implement them, and then wait for two years to start the same game again.

Modern organizations and the real leaders I've learned from during my various projects had one thing in common and dealt with differently. For all of them, this wasn't a one-time shot to get to the next level, followed by a long tail of increased entropy destroying all efficiency gains again. This is similar to a damped harmonic oscillator that will finally end up in the initial state. Instead, these leaders forced their organization to assimilate a continuous flow of change into their processes, organization, and underlying IT platforms to permanently reach the next level.

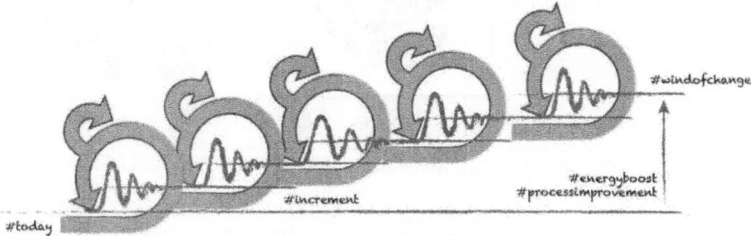

This also means their perfect marketing machine is never finished, and there are always ongoing improvements being brought in from outside of the enterprise (similar to external energy) to start fighting the disorder that appears every day, enforced by the natural law of thermodynamics.

One of the most prominent examples is corporate taxonomies and data cubes; with the advent of millions of data points in hundreds of databases and clouds, the need for some order is imminent.

Thus, most marketing departments that I've seen in the last 20 years have struggled with their campaign and paid, owned & earned execution power. Most of their time and efforts have been spent gathering data, normalizing them, and bringing them back into shiny reports and stories for their management. I've read a study on this (though I can't recall where but I think all of us know this is common sense) which stated 70% of the work is to collect and normalize data, 30% is to gain insights. Corporate taxonomies and data models overcome this burden, but due to the second law, an ongoing effort is necessary to focus your organization and make sure it stays in line with this model, and enhance it based on new requirements popping up every day within your enterprise.

As this ongoing flow of change is a key ingredient for me to become data-driven and to master the complex marketing technology stack, I've started developing a framework to give my clients a solid base for their continuous improvements. The intention has been to design a set of fundamental epics that will help a marketing manager, leader, and marketing department through the ongoing loops.

This is the framework below:

- Where am I — the DDM maturity assessment
- Where I'd like to be — design the next improvement
- Bridging the GAP — describing the field of actions
- Agile Implementation within the 3Ps: process, people, platforms/data

And again we sould to our mind the principles of the harmonic oscillator. Changing everthing at once is like a huge energy push into our IT, organizational and process setup. Newton's physical law of actio equal reactio will enforce our system of reference to go far beyond the point we orginially planned as perfect future to-be world. Just to collapse immediately to a lower level and finally oscillate around the new equilibrium. Be careful, use a continuous wind of change to transform your marketing to a new intelligent way of data-driven marketing.

To get there in this sense, I came up with the ma.tomics framework that's described in detail at the end of this book. The ma.tomics includes all the relevant topics we've seen above, the epics from the Gedankenexperiments, the Smart KPI framework, and the physical laws we've applied to data-driven marketing.

Solid State Physics — "building out complex systems"

The physics behind — large-scale properties

So, if we want to build a new intelligent data-driven marketing universe, we should ask the physicists: how does mother nature do this? What is the theory behind building solid blocks of material? This is the study of rigid matter or solids, through methods such as quantum mechanics, crystallography, electromagnetism, and metallurgy.

> "Solid-state physics studies how the large-scale properties of solid materials result from their atomic-scale properties."

Thus, solid-state physics forms a theoretical basis of materials science on top of atomic physics (which is similar to my ma.tomics framework). Many properties of materials are affected by their crystal structure. The properties of materials such as electrical conduction and heat capacity are also investigated by solid-state physics.

In other words, every part of this wonderful world is built out of less than 100 distinct atoms. Like a box of magic Lego bricks, it's possible to design nearly everything you can imagine out of this limited set of atoms. Each atom owns a different set of atomic-scale properties, which gives them a specific character.

Thus, solid-state physics teaches us about the possibility of designing and building complex systems out of simple parts. The challenging part is understanding the forces and interaction between these parts, as well as establishing and harvesting the knowledge about a unique combination of them to achieve the needs of your desired large-scale property.

In the real world of physics, we don't see isolated atoms existing for a long time. They tend to counteract with others to large-scale molecules, and properties. In the ecosystem of an enterprise, we see the same pattern.

What does this mean for marketing — competitive advantage

Coming back to the subject of marketing, I was thrilled at the idea of defining a similar elementary system of the main ma.tomics that allows every

CMO to design and establish their unique way of intelligent data-driven marketing setup. I came up with 18 ma.tomics, each representing a special topic, and split down into smaller sections. In total, a set of more than 50 different ma.tomics, allows us to transform marketing departments and helping them find a new, unique way of executing their processes, based on creativity, data, and budget.

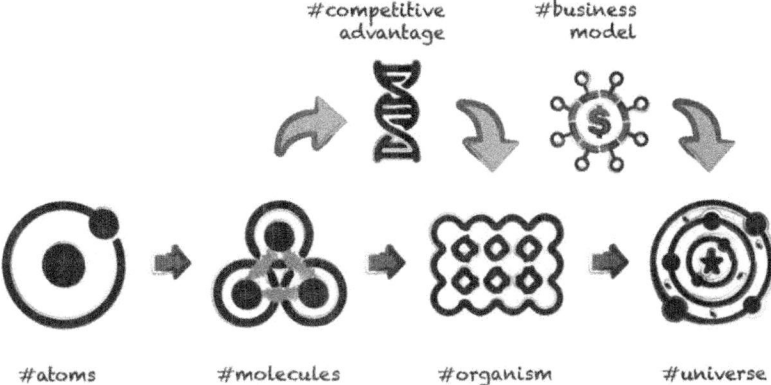

At the beginning of this book, I referenced (Porter, 1985): "Enterprises that can engineer and transform their different departments in a closed-loop engine to plan, prepare, execute and control all paid, owned and earned marketing activities and touch-points will gain a competitive advantage." Referring back to that point, then I believe that a system can't be easily copied by your competition.

For me, solid-state physics and the ma.tomics framework is the ultimate way to reach this goal. While the ingredients like "getting audience-centric and customer-focused," "marketing taxonomy," "hyper-accurate targeting and look-a-like" etc., (for more information, see the chapter about the framework at the end of this book) are open to everyone, the individual combination and deep implementation within your organization and processes are going to give you a competitive advantage.

If there would be a general one-size-fits-all blueprint for intelligent data-driven marketing, this would no longer be a competitive advantage. The only things you need to do are read, plan, and implement the solution shown in the blueprint. But this isn't strictly true; business models, strategic audiences, customer behaviors, and markets for every enterprise, define a different universe. Your intelligent data-driven marketing set up needs to fit into this universe, otherwise, you'll fail!

I'm quite lucky as I was allowed to help one of my clients over more than 15 years. Within that time, we were always transforming their habits and capabilities, directing them toward a fully implemented, data-driven marketing system. The client is one of the world's most famous advertisers and, sometimes, honored as the inventor of the storytelling and branded content marketing approach. What we learned together over this long period is that the ongoing need for new energy in form of change and innovation (flow of change — see above) combined with a clear set of topics that need to be developed to a new level of maturity, will push you in front of your competitors, and allow you to run a high performing marketing machine far beyond the competition.

The layers of this large-scale property were quite simple. As always, what looks like a simple process at the end, is a tough journey to implement. In a mixed team of marketing, IT, and experienced consultants, we established a unique way of consequent ingesting of all consumer touchpoints into a single data management and customer data platform similar to what is described in our Gedankenexperiment 2.0 above. And if I say all, I mean all; the lake was filled with every event data from anonymous visits on their website, their newsletters, their bots, ticket sales for brand building and sponsor events, WIFI-hotpot login data, app usage, buying behaviors in their point of sales, consumer activation campaigns based on QR codes, and beacons, etc.

This means there were two to three digits of millions of data points per day being mined! This was the foundation for an enterprise-wide data model, analysis, and behavioral driven segmentation.

The last layer was the full-blown re-integration into each activation layer, so you can target people in a personalized way and recommend the next best action as well as branded content in the most fitting demand window. Behind-the-scenes means to integrate all front-facing, customer office systems, like the web, mobile CMS, the shop, the chat, and social bots, the newsletter and text messsage system, their demand-side platforms, the hardware for WIFI-hotspots, the trade-promotion systems, and point of sale cashier systems, etc.

But as Isaak Newton stated, "action = reaction." There's a large trade-off you need to consider upon starting your transformation program. Clayton Christenson (Christensen, 1997) has shaped this idea in his theory about disruptive innovations and the challenge of being imprisoned within a high performing organization, and processes.

Such a transformation also enforces you to develop your organization and have specialist roles, which you can combine uniquely. This setup is highly resistant against change and also people tend to work in silos on dedicated topics instead of becoming skilled in various disciplines. For that reason, you need to carefully balance the law of thermodynamics and the theory of solid-state physics to stay competitive over a long period on the market. Just remember: the amplitude of a harmonic oscillation is highly affected by the counter forces within the inertial system of reference.

Einstein's Theory of Relativity — "There is one last thing"

The Physics Behind: The Theory of Relativity

You followed my thoughts and experiments now for more than 90 sites, and so far, we're only missing one fundamental piece of marketing. I've put this at the end of my thoughts, in the hopes that this may help you to remember it on top of all the other insights. Albert Einstein, in his theory of special relativity, determined that the laws of physics are the same for all non-accelerating observers. He showed that the speed of light within a vacuum is the same no matter what observers travel.

$$E = m * c^2$$

In other words, the ultimate speed is dubbed light speed and all other topics must be seen and calculated relative to it. This also includes from the perspective of a static observer running watches tick a bit slower than their one. The effect is called "time dilatation."

If a book gets published by physicists who've been thinking about marketing, it's assumed there must be a chapter about Albert Einstein and his theories. The longer I'm involved in this ecosystem of intelligent data-driven marketing, the more I see the need for an ultimate light-speed definition here.

Besides data and budget, creativity in marketing is the main factor for a successful marketing campaign.

Maybe it is a good moment to combine the theory of the most famous physicist with some wise words from management theory 'Pope' Peter Drucker: "There are marketing and innovation within a company, all the rest are costs." Both innovation and creativity in marketing will generate new customers, and help to attract existing ones to convert to long-term friends and fans.

What Does This Mean for Marketing? Creativity is Still King

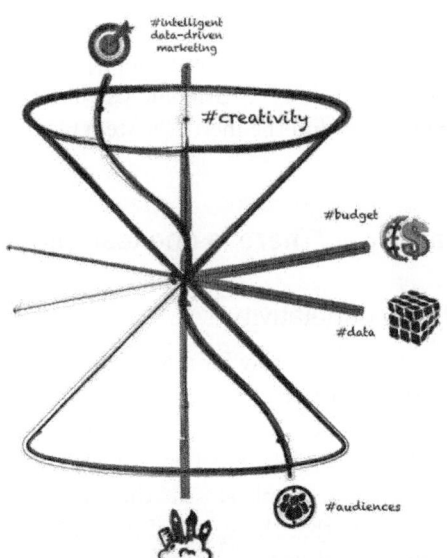

As said above, in this ecosystem of perfectly planned and orchestrated paid, owned, earned campaigns, and journeys, a marketing technology stack where nearly everything and everybody can be measured and an organization that relies 100% on data instead of gut feeling, there's a strong need to add a third ingredient to the perfect marketing machine.

I've once had a workshop with the invitation slogan, "From mad-men to math-men." After two intensive days of collaborative working, we all agreed that creativity is still the light speed that separates the leaders from the laggards.

What was also obvious, is that there's no way of running good marketing without data. It looks like these two things are bound, like mass and light speed in Einstein's famous formula. I will come back to this a little later in this book.

However, Einstein's theory is not only about the ultimate speed of light, but the direct consequence of this is also that time is relative.

Depending on the speed of your inertial system of reference to another, a second is longer or shorter.

The faster you run, the longer your seconds are spread. Wow, so what does this mean for our closed-loop and agile marketing setup? The faster we can run in agile iterations, the more time we have! I think there isn't a better motivation for the audience and data-driven closed-loop marketing. If you can run with half of the speed of light, you have double as much time as your competitor standing still on his historic way of doing classic waterfall planning and context-specific marketing.

For me, Einstein's theory and other physical laws helped to understand the complexity of marketing systems. This is slightly similar to Eliyahu Goldratt (Goldratt, 2004) who once observed his kids on a boy scout trip walking in a straight line. His observations and findings ultimately ended up in the Theory of "Lean Management." The more I've used this analogy of physics and marketing, the more parallels between the two spring to mind and are discovered. Let me finish this chapter with my favorite parallel.

The Physics Behind — The General Theory of Relativity

General relativity, also known as the general theory of relativity, is the geometric theory of gravitation and the current description of gravitation in modern physics. General relativity enhances special relativity and refines Newton's law of universal gravitation, which therefore provides a unified description of gravity as a geometric property of space and time. In particular, the curvature of space and time is directly related to the energy and momentum of whatever matter and radiation are present in that moment.

$$R_{\mu\nu} + \frac{1}{2} R g_{\mu\nu} = \frac{8\pi G}{c^4} * T_{\mu\nu}$$

Some predictions of general relativity differ significantly from those of classical physics, especially the propagation of light. The predictions of general relativity linked to classical physics have been confirmed in all observations and experiments to date.

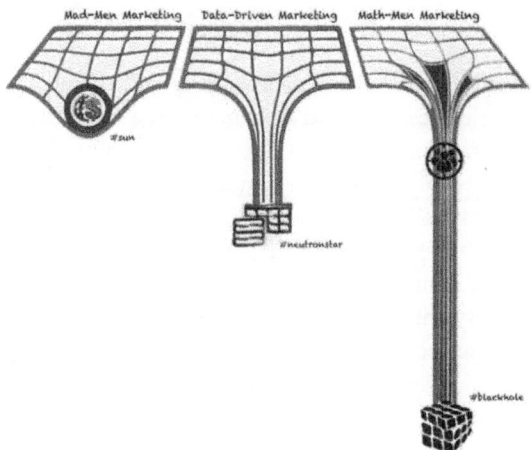

Einstein's theory has important astrophysical implications. For example, it implies the existence of black holes — regions of space in which space and time are distorted in such a way that nothing — not even light — can escape. The bending of light due to gravity can lead to the phenomenon of gravitational lensing, in which multiple images of the same distant astronomical object are visible in the sky. General relativity also predicts the existence of gravitational waves. Furthermore, general relativity is the basis of current cosmological models of a consistently expanding universe.

What Does This Mean for Marketing? Data Matters

My goodness, this is a lot to wrap your head around so I do hope you are still with me and remain curious enough to follow this last liaison between the miracles of physics and implications in marketing. Let us run through the general theory of relativity and analyze the different parts.

First, we see the evidence that there are gravitation waves in between two massive matters and the gravitational lensing. Consider the data as if it were a planet or another object with sufficient mass (McCrory, 2010). As the data accumulates (builds mass) there is a greater likelihood that additional services and applications will be attracted to this data. This is the same effect that gravity has on objects around a planet or sun. As the mass or density increases, so does the strength of the gravitational pull. As things draw closer to the mass, they accelerate toward it at a faster velocity that increases as the object draws ever nearer to that mass.

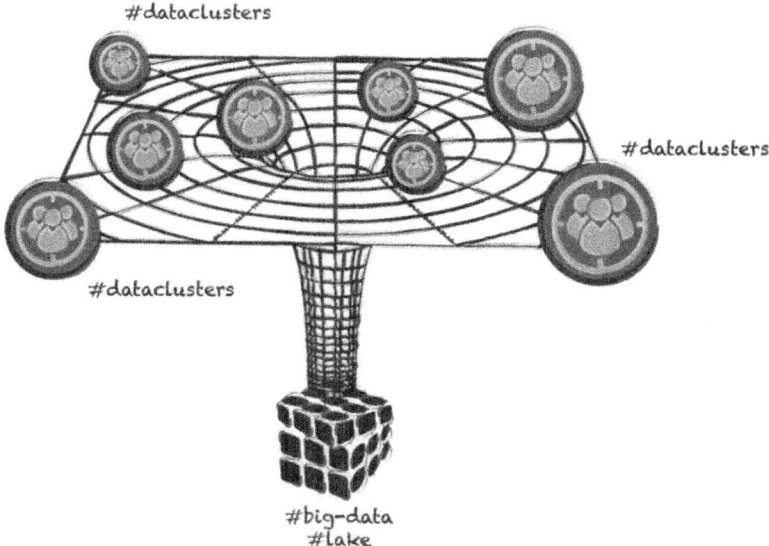

It means the more data that exists in a given source or repository, the greater its perceived value. Software and services are brought to the data as a means of exploiting its value. Similarly, the greater the amount of data, the more other data might be connected to it, which would, as a result, increase its value for the analytics.

I'm sure you are aware of what I'm speaking about here; a tiny set of aggregated data is normally of low value, but building broader repositories of well-structured and audience-centric data increases the value significantly. Once the initial effort of bringing together the first big data chunks is done, positive network effects will then establish an entry barrier to new market incumbents and save the data sovereignty. For example, Google, the most popular search engine, Netflix, the leading online video streaming service, Facebook, the global social network, and Amazon, the biggest online retailer have all shown us this in various, impressive ways.

The propagation of light can teach us two things. One thing is that only huge amounts of data are capable of changing the direction of light. Remember we used light and light speed as the replacement for creativity in marketing? For me, this is exactly what represents the perfect marketing machine I've stated often in this book. You can use the data to change the way creativity has worked on the early day of mad-men marketing and it can also be used to change the effect and representation of your marketing slightly.

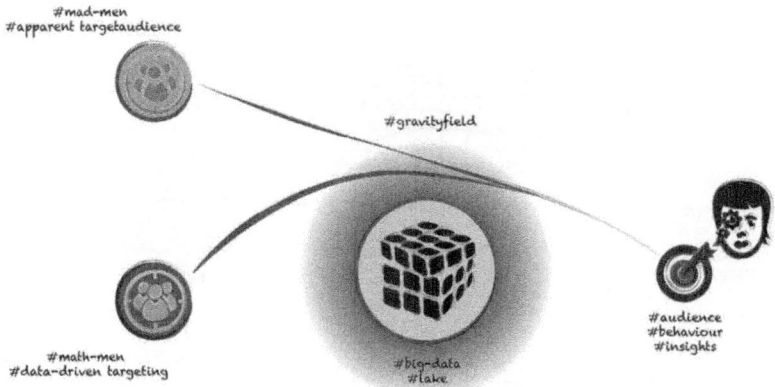

But if we think further ahead, we end up at the theory about black holes that can completely deflect light. A black hole just burns every creativity by the sheer amount of data it has. Closed advertising business models spring to my mind that is based on billions of data points. The endless amount of social postings, hashtags, behavioral click paths, and behavioral patterns of modern social networks in combination with their way of acting as a wallet garden looks like a real black hole in the current marketing universe.

Finally, let's touch upon the subject of the constantly expanding universe. Twenty years ago, when I first started in marketing consulting, the universe was quite easy. With the advent of digital ways of advertising and the further inclusion of owned activations into the marketeers possibilities, now we end up with more than 8000 marketing platforms and tools you need to master as a state-of-the-art CMO (Brinker, 2020).

Einstein's theory just reminds us that the marketing universe will never rest and the current strategies of how to market are not always reliable and no longer pursue innovations. The fast-evolving and innovative industry, the massive amount of money spent on marketing (according to Statista 625 Billion Dollar), the implications of data protection rules, and the fact that awareness generation for every business model are the first steps in business and lead generation, and they are the driving force of this ongoing expansion of the marketing universe.

That concludes the first part of this book. In the next section, we delve further and view more than 20 years of condensed data-driven marketing knowledge in-depth and that is the ma.tomics framework.

The ma.tomics — Intelligent Data-Driven Marketing Framework

If we have a look at "A Brief History of Humankind" (Harari, 2014), we will see that around 13.5 billion years ago, matter, energy, time, and space came into being in what is known as the Big Bang. The story of these fundamental features of our universe is called physics. Approximately 300,000 years after their appearance, matter and energy started to coalesce into complex structures called atoms, which then combined into what's known as molecules. The story of atoms, molecules, and their interactions is called chemistry. Around 3.8 billion years ago, on our planet, Earth, certain molecules combined to form particularly large and intricate structures called organisms. The story of organisms and their formation is called biology. Roughly 70,000 years ago, organisms belonging to the species homo sapiens formed more elaborate structures called cultures. The subsequent development of these human cultures is called history.

Several centuries ago, people learned to generate demand for their products and brands by promising them to dedicated audiences with an attractive price and warm words called promotions. The story of this way of influencing others is called Marketing.

The purpose of the intelligent data-driven marketing (DDM) framework "ma.tomics" is to dissect the decomposition of the complex setup of contemporary marketing departments to separate and loosely couple atomic-sized elements. The framework enables people to manage the digital transformation of the current marketing processes, the enablement of the organization, and mastering marketing IT platforms in tiny pieces and steps to finally bring this together in a new comprehensive solid system based on the gravity waves that represent fundamental skills and habits to interconnect all the ma.tomics. While each ma.tomic can be implemented and enhanced individually, the defined framework gravity waves help to arrange and combine the single ma.tomic to a state of the art and modern and intelligent data-driven marketing approach.

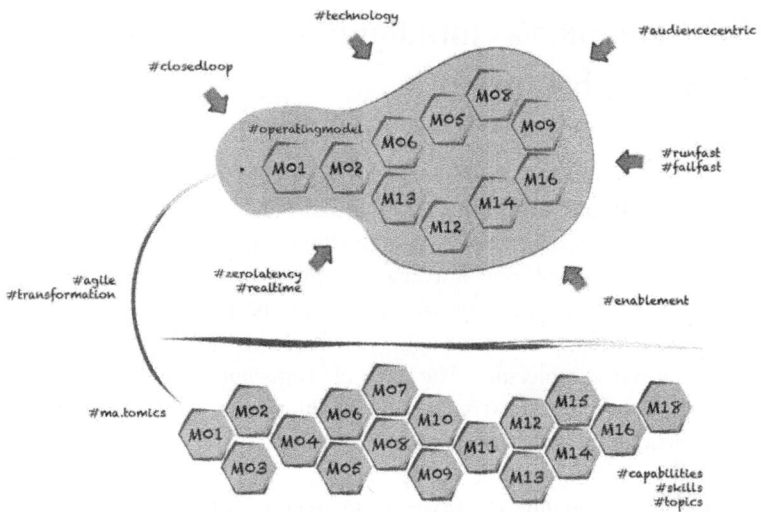

So **ma.tomics** means building **marketing** out of independent and loosely coupled **atoms**. The result is a marketing universe that is based on an agile target operating model, heavily supported by cloud-based IT platforms that provide a 100% personalized customer experience and service.

Let us start with the six fundamental gravity waves that bring more than 50 following ma.tomics together. This can be seen as the magic glue in-between the different ma.tomics each representing an independent capability of your organization, process, and IT marketing ecosystem.

GW1 From counting actions to guiding audiences

Gravity wave one is the paradigm of going from mad-men towards the math-men; I hope you remember the development from pure use of creativity and budget via the counting of actions like impressions and clicks towards the ability to follow your audience through the marketing universe and guide them within user journeys to the next best actions based on past behavior.

Data points will cease to be counting content usage or delivery like impressions, clicks, views. Instead, intelligent data-driven marketing allows to measure, store and report each customer touchpoint based on audience-centric data cubes (e.g. reach1+, clickers, viewers) which are based on big data platforms.

For that reason, we should take into consideration the fundamental maturity level increases whenever we are implementing any combination of ma.tomics. Start with the easy-to-use and consume context centric counting and activation. From there, you can then enter the complex world of managing audiences and guiding them based on the behavior you can see in your data and the predictions of your intelligent algorithms.

This also implies the heavy use of big data platforms and predictive frameworks on the IT layer. Becoming audience-centric means straying away from aggregated data and taking the single user interaction as the most granular piece of data and the new normal. As we'd like to follow our audience this also means dealing with the ability to merge the captured data to comprehensive profiles while dancing with the tiger around the legal and legitimate constraints of data protection.

GW2 Real-time and zero latency

The second gravity wave comes directly from dealing with huge amounts of data in big data architectures. We need a fundamental paradigm that states, once data are generated, they are available in near-realtime to the full system. Otherwise, most of the use-cases like negative segments in programmatic ad activations or real-time experience personalization will never work properly. Data needs to be available in real-time to be rendered on standard reports on defined status dates, to frequently update our explorative data cubes, and to answer as quickly as possible the hypothesis via highly skilled data scientists.

Again we see the high demand for the latest IT infrastructure that has a good application framework and an open API interface availability. Only the direct and access without any latency time allows us to take advantage of real audience-centric data-driven marketing. Otherwise, we are falling back into the world of aggregated and context centric data cubes that are full of old data that just allows us to do some kind of growth hacking through descriptive analysis.

Within our ma.tomics implementation, this gravity wave is not purely focussed on the best leverage of the IT infrastructure. There are also fields of action on processes and an organizational level to guarantee a zero-latency, agile way of executing marketing so that you can master the fast-moving change of the marketing universe.

GW3 Closed-Loop — Harmonic Oscillation

The third gravity wave focuses more on the way we execute and design our processes within an intelligent data-driven marketing setup. The overarching goal is to orchestrate all ma.tomics in a closed loop that allows you to plan, prepare, execute, measure, and predict your marketing strategy, programs and campaigns. We have seen that closed loops, combined with energizing forces, will lead us to a harmonic oscillation around a better new equilibrium. All our doing and the way we combine and implement the ma.tomics should rely on this ongoing plan to measure and optimize flow to reach higher levels of efficiency and effectiveness, and to foster the most creative way of attracting our audiences.

GW4 Mastering the Tech-Stack-Orchestration

May the fourth be with you! See what we did there? The next gravity wave was mentioned partly in previous chapters. There is no way of running intelligent marketing without mastering the full technology stack. The CMO looks like the new CIO as he needs to invest heavily in big data frameworks, planning and workflow platforms, and marketing clouds.

Without mastering the marketing technology stack each DDM initiative is built to fail. In addition to the owned marketing infrastructure, integration of external marketing and Ad-Tech platforms like Google, Facebook, Microsoft, Tencent, etc. is key. The fast-moving world in this domain is quite tricky; to stay vigilant in case of any daily surprises caused by data leaks (remember the Cambridge Analytica scandal?), new laws and endless creative innovations are challenges that can't be overcome without a deep understanding of the underlying IT constraints and possibilities.

For that reason, my advice is to understand the fundamental IT topics, rules, constraints, and innovations of the marketing technology stack and what cloud or framework is necessary to fulfill your requirements. Instead of digging into the nitty-gritty details of every new marketing technology every CMO and his team should invest in tech-savvy colleagues who can follow the market and shape innovations and disruptions.

While most enterprises I've seen in the last few years who had various marketing transformation projects were just using the newest tools the leaders mastered to challenge and combine them to give them a competitive advantage; they did this by adding two isolated pieces together to get something more valuable. Ma.tomics helps you to understand the need for IT support and how to leverage the benefits of multi-cloud marketing technology stacks.

GW5 Run Agile — Start Fast and Fail Fast

The underlying process of marketing has not changed over the last 2000 years; we still collect, analyze, segment, activate, and collaborate data to find out which investment is worth and which is waste. John Wannamaker declared the rule nearly 200 years ago but it still applies to the marketing universe today. However, the speed of innovation and complexity increased so fast that the old way of marketing (by allocating marketing, asking for marketing partners, defining the strategy and execution in one single push to the market) no longer works. We have seen, over the last few years, the advent of audience-driven marketing with the possibility to (re-) target your most promising prospects through programmatic advertising, just to directly be followed by a phase of data protection laws and the deprecation of 3rd party cookies. In parallel to previously, we moved away from pure performance and product marketing towards storytelling and brand management to find out that our eCommerce business works better once supported with clear call-to-actions in focused digital performance campaigns.

Even if you can follow the seemingly endless innovations and trends, you will never be able to rest as the half-time value of the knowledge of winning 50% of your marketing is too short. Intelligent data-driven marketing can't be implemented in a single waterfall project approach. Instead, steady development of each ma.tomic as well as a continuous orchestration and optimization of all of them in subsequent sprints is the winning formula. Similar to the massive A/B testing of your activations, you should also start working on the underlying backbone that is your marketing processes, organization, and IT infrastructure. I've seen many CMOs talking about the need for more agility and flexibility, I've rarely seen any company being able to implement a true "run fast, fail fast" strategy, which means allowing parts of your marketing activations to fail. The final goal is to optimize the parts with the lowest investment and highest return in a 100% open and data-driven way. I know all of you reading this book will agree with me that this is the right approach but the question remains: are you acting like this when running and guiding your marketing departments and external agencies?

Let me bring up here a really funny story from a long time ago; we were sitting in the US headquarter in Los Angeles of a well-known global big advertiser.

The client was admired for his marketing ecosystem and his approach of 100% storytelling that he applied instead of pure product advertising. Part of the ecosystem was a new video portal and app to promote the massive video library they have set up during the last years. We had a meeting with the agency that was in charge of the "new app campaign" and my job was to bring in the numbers into the game. It was the first time that the client used his analytics instead of relying on the agency's reporting. Our funnel was quite clear and within the briefing of the CMO I've shown that we see a cost per action (CPA) for a single download of $950. You can imagine the following meeting with the agency managers did not run very smoothly. The agency showed the numbers of downloads and argued that even if the numbers had not reached the final goal, the campaign itself was very successful as the awareness was far beyond the expected reach. The CMO was not amused and finally came up with the idea next time to buy some pre-installed iPhones and give them away for free on the 2nd street of Santa Monica. That would be much cheaper and will generate at least the same amount of installed apps and a lot of publicity.

The interesting part for me was not the fact that it was quite clear data-driven marking is transparent and successful, it was the reaction of the agency manager in the meeting. They started to argue about awareness, success, future investments, campaign attribution effects, etc. instead of being honest about a fucked-up campaign. On the other side of the table, the client's marketing team wasn't willing to accept that this expensive and thoroughly selected agency failed. For me, it looked like the client's marketing management thought that if they agreed the agency failed and the CMO is here, this will directly fall back onto them and show that they are also not successful. Nobody talked about the huge insights we first time gained by really tracking audience-centric data in a DMP and the possibilities to see why we had that high bounce rates resp. low app download rates. The CMO, nor his management, or the agency, was able to run fast and fail fast. They burned the total seven-digit campaign budget in a single rush just to see that the concept has not shown any return on the pre-aligned success KPIs of cost per download.

For that reason run fast and fail fast means shaping the way you worked in the past, how you dealt with your partners and how you managed success within your organization. It also means going away from waterfall models and going towards an interactive way of executing campaigns.

Using the ma.tomics means also implementing change rapidly to show a role model of agility and show how to run in short interactions towards a common clear and measurable goal.

GW6 Enable the organization

We have seen gravity waves that help to understand the need to move towards audience-centric marketing, to tackle new technology skills, the ability to run agile marketing in sprint setups, and to understand that only closed-loop process management instead of historic waterfall approaches will win in the future.

Keeping in mind the constant increase of entropy and the need for a steady stream of energy to avoid the chaos of your ecosystem should help us to define another fundamental capability of our new marketing universe. All the IT and processes don't work if the people involved are not behaving in the way you designed it. But being human means also being an independent thinker with the ability to follow your thoughts and strategies. It means we need a creative way of enabling our people's skills and habits and form them in a way that we finally move towards our common goal of being completely data-driven.

Helping your organization to adopt these data-driven habits, capabilities, and skills of each talent by pursuing the different teams through the maturity levels of educating, changing, exciting, and executing is the last gravity wave that combines the different parts of the ma.tomics framework.

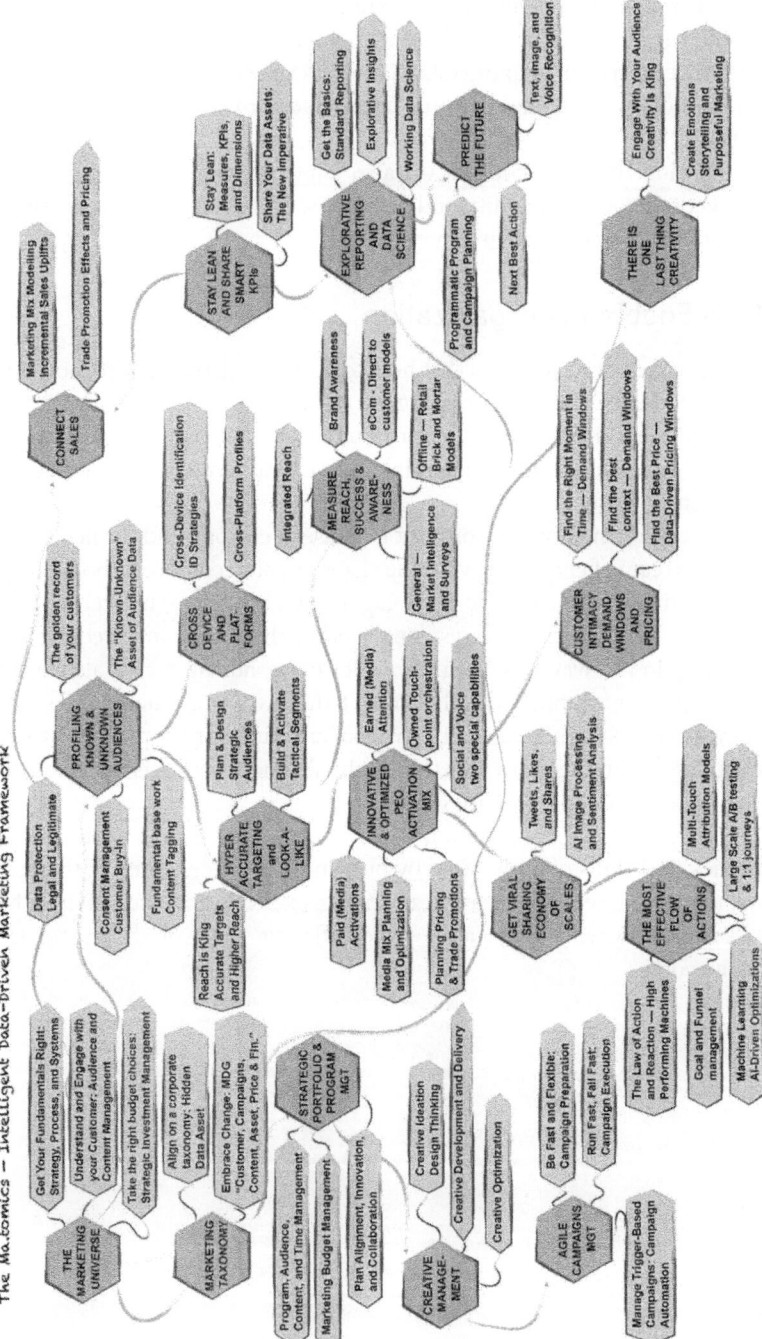

M1 THE MARKETING UNIVERSE

The fundamental direction of a marketing strategy that includes processes, organization, and technology is the foundation for successful marketing execution. This ma.tomic also includes defining the overall audience and content strategy as well as the strategic budget management; it is essentially the comprehensive blueprint of your definition of "intelligent marketing."

M1.1 Get Your Fundamentals Right: Strategy, Process, and Systems

This ma.tomic should help you to define the areas and possibilities you can influence as well as describe the constraints and burdens you cannot overcome or even exclude dedicated topics, organizational units, or systems from your system of reference for data-driven marketing.

This will then define your strategy on approaching the market, and it also includes the operational organization and process domains (e.g. brand marketing, customer interaction, analytics and insights, creative development, sponsoring, event management, etc.). You need to set up an innovative, agile marketing universe.

This first part of your marketing strategy and vision is focusing more on the "what" — what is the right content, audience, and brand I need to achieve the highest return? Within this includes finding the balance of investing into brand awareness and direct performance campaigns with a clear call to action. The second part delves more into the pragmatic parts of planning and executing the overall agile marketing closed-loop program and campaign management. While the first part was the "what" this part is the "how" — how do I design and implement a working process and organization to leverage my winning content?

The third and final section is the "why" — why is this setup and content (not) working? Hopefully, you will have insights from the millions of data points as the "why" is the strategy of turning mountains of data into valuable insights.

Now that we have summarized the sections before you begin, ensure you have a clear image of your marketing universe — both as it is now and what you want it to be. Without these foundations, the transformation will fail for sure.

Impact

- The overall understanding of current marketing strategies and the lean design of a better and data-driven marketing universe will help you to focus on the core things that need to be changed. It will also prevent you from doing the "wrong" things and therefore reduce spend on marketing because you won't have had many failed attempts.

Fields of Actions

- Analyze the current way you are doing marketing within a SWOT analysis.
- Define the data-driven and intelligent vision of your future marketing blueprint
- Compare both with a GAP analysis.
- Define the initial focus areas, stories with high value and low effort will set up your first backlog for the future transformation program.
- Collect and analyze the existing data pots to prove your blueprint and hypothesis with real data and aggregate them in a business case for your transformation program.

IT Support & Platforms

- This ma.tomic is not supported by real marketing IT platforms; most of the work can be done in standard office products, process design tools, and Kanban boards.

M1.2 Understand and Engage with your Customer: Audience and Content Management

Once the overall marketing approach has been designed and aligned, it's time for this ma.tomic, which includes the people you like to engage with. It means to analyze and define who your target is, which is the most unpredictable factor. It also deals with the definition of your strategic audiences and translation into several target groups (audiences) that you can reach within your marketing universe.

Based on the understanding of the customer's generic moods, habits, and behaviors, you will be able to cluster them into different strategic audiences and correlated customer journeys.

Within the classic marketing mix, we would argue that the previous ma.tomic is related to the two P's: promotion and product. However, promotion only regards the way we like to interact with our target groups. This ma.tomic is the place and the second part of the promotion P: the winning content.

The most relevant content topics and stories need to be analyzed and defined, so they can be packed into a program backlog that is input for the following program and portfolio management ma.tomic.

Impact

- The definition of strategic audiences and related target groups allow running targeted campaigns with less wasted investments.
- Effective user journey and high converting target groups build the foundation for a real customer experience with maximized efficiency.
- Personalized content and target group-specific next best action recommendations will maximize your funnel conversions (efficiency).

Fields of Actions

- Build personas and user journeys, while including a touch-point analysis where you can interact with each target group.
- Map persona — journeys — audience/target groups in a matrix.
- Identify, analyze, connect and consume first second, and third-party data sources.
- Analyze your marketing audiences by running: Reach, Overlap/Skew, and Ecosystem analysis.
- Analyze the current consumption of your online content, including bounce rates and click paths.
- Run content ideas and tests.

IT Support and Platforms

- DMP, CDP, and social listening platforms to understand customer behavior, moods, and needs.
- Web, mobile, and social analytic platforms to understand the content usage and conversions.
- Real-time interaction analytic platforms (Sankey click paths) to understand the flow of users within your owned ecosystem.

- Access to data broker platforms and data partners to enhance your customer profiles.
- Cluster and correlation analysis/algorithms to find hidden data patterns.

M1.3 Take the right budget choices: Strategic Investment Management

A well-balanced investment in brand awareness, innovation and markets, infrastructure and technology skills, trade promotions, customer equity, and experience, etc. will distinguish your marketing approach from the competition and set you apart from the rest.

As one of the three key ingredients for intelligent data-driven marketing, the budget is your essential blood keeping your machine running. While the easy game is just to increase the budget to see higher results the intelligent way is to wisely invest in the channels, formats, and activations that will generate the highest return on investment.

While classic marketing budgets mostly contain only the activation costs, production costs, and the internal headcounts, new approaches have elected to include the technology costs for the marketing technology stack, the activation and promotion costs on the sales side, and all efforts related to the customer experience on owned platforms in the marketing budgeting.

Having seen dozens of different budgeting processes, I'm convinced there's one way of spreading the money within your organization best; It has to be a perfect balance and be a strictly centrally organized waterfall process that allocates money to the big buckets from the top down. There is also the need for a perfectly fitting bottom-up process following agile rules to use the money in interactive short sprints to generate maximum return on investment in parallel with the highest flexibility to react to market and customer changes.

Due to the volatile and agile environment, there may be a need to revise the budget within a planning cycle regularly to stay in line with the customer needs and follow the agile marketing approach in the campaign execution.

This ma.tomic also includes following the 70-20-10 rule, which means investing 70% of your budget into well-known formats and channels. The 20% should be used for new ways of doing the working that is offered by the marketing. The last 10% should be used to develop your way of activations and the best ways to get into contact with your audience.

Impact

- The consideration of all cost drivers (paid, owned, earned), including the production cost and sales promotions to allow a real and comprehensive ROMI.
- Regularly revise cycles, including feedback from accountable parties. This allows us to be agile towards the customer. This flexibility opens the possibility to act with the highest effectiveness.

Fields of Actions

- Design a global budgeting process and strategy by combining top-down and centrally steered budgeting rounds with ongoing and agile iterations of bottom-up planning.
- Define all relevant cost drivers and map them into one planning system for all involved organizational units.
- Install an overall enterprise-wide taxonomy to allocate cost towards programs, campaigns, and activations (plan/actual).
- Resolve the impediment that finance has to close the month/year in comparison to marketing that allocates to the month they bought impressions.
- Use the 70-20-10 rule that spreads the budget across different domains of known, new, and unique ways of connecting with your audience.

IT Support & Platforms

- Marketing resource management and planning platform to set up and maintain one central campaign planning database.
- Integration into the existing finance world by connecting to the companies general ledger and necessary sub-ledgers within the enterprise resource planning cloud (ERP)

M2 MARKETING TAXONOMY

The second ma.tomic domain deals with implementing a consolidated canonical data model and rollout into the comprehensive enterprise. The canonical model enables the gathering and analysis of marketing-related data to generate insights without the necessity to normalize all the data every time and to maintain the endless amounts of mapping tables. Continuous taxonomy maintenance and clear database governance are keys to success; they are also part of the IT support.

M2.1 Align on a corporate taxonomy: Hidden Data Asset

Taking both parts of intelligent data-driven marketing means dealing with data to gain competitive intelligence and advantage. Hence, the data structure that shows how to store used objects like marketing plans, initiatives or programs, campaigns, providers, customers, etc. is a hidden asset. Modern marketing takes care of a large number of insights as a basis for customer insights, predictive models, and programmatic campaign activations.

The main challenge that presents itself in most cases is designing a metamodel, which is some kind of canonical data model. This allows you to run your algorithms, generate insights and recommendations on a more general structure and puts the mapping of real data out of hundreds of data pots apart from this. This means the enterprise spanning consolidation of the structure of how to store all data points opens the possibility for non-limited analytics and an easier way to share data and insights. This also saves time because there is no longer a need to extract, transform, and load for each analysis data from the various data sources.

Impact

- A consolidated enterprise taxonomy allows us to easily find correlations between KPIs in all kinds of dimensions. This is more efficient and therefore saves time seeing as everybody acts on the same foundation.
- The filled taxonomy is the fundamental base for all predictive models and programmatic activations that will increase the return on investment by using the best actions and personalizations.

Fields of Actions

- Define the fundamental measures (not KPIs) and where to find them in the underlying source system(s) within a data, touchpoint, system matrix.
- Align on core and optional dimensions and guarantee to get them for all defined measures.
- Align on a small set of common KPIs and their calculation logic and naming governance.
- Take care about the difference between audience and content-centric measures and KPIs.
- Cluster data as 1st, 2nd, and 3rd-party data and profile data into non-PII/PII relevant.

IT Support & Platforms

- Default canonical data models for marketing cloud (plans, programs, campaigns, customers, leads, opportunities, assets, etc.).
- DMP and CDP tagging of ads, sites, apps, bots, and other content.

M2.2 Embrace Change: Master Data Governance "Customer, Campaigns, Content, Asset, Price & Finance"

Once defined, designed, and in place, an enterprise-wide taxonomy in form of a canonical data model for customers, campaigns, content, assets, etc. is a living beast that needs to be fed every single day. Remember the law of thermodynamics; without proper maintenance in the form of extra energy, the disorder will increase in our universe! For that reason, we need to install special master data governance (MDG) and have a more defined way of doing it the once defined taxonomy can be changed and enhanced. To cover the business part of defining the new requirements of KPIs and dimensions, the technical part of the implementation, and the organizational part of enabling your organization to all these changes.

Defined master data management (MDM) processes have to be implemented to maintain the existing structure in a controlled workflow and to follow strict rules for any change requests of the existing marketing taxonomy.

Scenario-based patterns like e.g. a new country/market, new product, pricing changes, product launches, etc. can be defined and implemented within the master data management platforms to guarantee consistent data across the organization and platforms.

Impact

- Without an MDM/MDG process in place, enterprise taxonomies will be snapshots and therefore outdated as soon as they are launched. The advantage of fast data intelligence will erode and the efficiency burned.
- MDM/MDG processes define clear responsibilities for all measures, dimensions, and KPIs including the underlying IT source systems that help to train specialists with competitive skills and to enable the organization to take advantage of this.

Fields of Actions

- Design data responsibly and the way to change the taxonomy (marketing MDM/MDG processes).
- Design scenarios to set up datasets (e.g. a new campaign) in all related systems.
- Design and implement a clear responsibility map (RACI) for data domains within the taxonomy.

IT Support and Platforms

- Special MDM and MDG platforms help to stay on top of your canonical data model.
- API frameworks and cloud allow you to connect to existing platforms and provide comprehensive server-to-server integrations.

M3 STRATEGIC PORTFOLIO & PROGRAM MANAGEMENT

This next domain of ma.tomics covers the way we structure our marketing activities into campaigns and clustering them into a break-down structure of plans, programs, and portfolios. While the CMO is mostly interested in organizing his activations across the globe on a timescale, the CFO is more interested in how to integrate into the general finance structure to control investment and brand value within the P&L and balance sheet.

M3.1 Program, Audience, Content, and Time Management

You should recall that the number of measures in our system of reference is limited. On the other hand, the dimensions look quite broad, so there's so much need to focus on a clear structure of this part. We had the ma.tomic of a corporate-wide taxonomy defining the measures of the overarching structure we'd like to do our planning rounds in.

Consequently, it's time to define a ma.tomic dealing with the planning process. On top of the campaign, we finally run in a single marketing area so there's some kind of superstructure that helps us to aggregate our measures within programs and portfolios. It all begins with an idea of a CMO that will be step-by-step split into distinctive marketing programs thoroughly distributed over the next planning period. The superstructure helps us also to define the marketing mix for several campaigns by dealing with different kinds of audiences (strategic and tactical audiences) that are finally reflected within activation segments in our campaigns and the necessary content.

This way of waterfall planning focuses on the topics that need to be placed in the marketing universe and markets via dedicated push campaigns and automatically triggered journeys.

To summarize, each of these programs defines the goals and strategy for the planned audiences to be reached, the funnel or journey, the budget (mix), and a rough timeframe to be on air with different campaigns within the programs. This also means the programs define the demand for new marketing assets to be produced before the campaigns start, though creative demand is part of the next ma.tomic domain.

Impact

- A more static and top-down driven way of planning marketing programs allows us to build a superstructure and grid for future agile preparation and execution.
- The holistic planning of goals, timelines, and topics guarantees a non-overlapping continuous way of addressing audiences and markets with the highest effectiveness.
- Programs allow us to aggregate reach and performance measures across several campaigns and activations within a single user journey.

Fields of Actions

- Establish a "beyond pure budgeting" marketing program planning (fixed timeframes or rolling planning), beginning with a strategic key-note from the CMO, through a more top-down program planning down to a bottom-up campaign planning.
- Establish the change of top-down thinking in programs to a combined portfolio with agile campaign execution and automation via user journeys.
- Align on the essential attributes and dimensions of defining a marketing program, campaign, and activation.

IT Support and Platforms

- Marketing resource management and planning platforms.

M3.2 Marketing Budget Management

While the previous ma.tomic M1.3 has dealt with the overall allocation of strategic investments within the marketing universe, this ma.tomic focuses on synchronizing the finance and marketing world and also establish a comprehensive and globally aligned budgeting process. To establish trust in the evidence of marketing success, direct integration into the financial budgeting processes and systems (enterprise finance) is key for successful strategic marketing planning.

While the old fashioned style of managing your marketing activations is to solely spread the budgets top-down, the modern way is vice versa. The starting point is to define your marketing goals with the question: what does it take to reach these goals? Intelligent data-driven algorithms will allow you to calculate the necessary investment per program and campaign based on historic insights and future predictions. The final derived budgets will be summarized in the different marketing programs, plans, and portfolios. These programs and plans are the foundation for the following bottom-up approach and will automatically be pushed over into the finance world (P&L within finance and controlling) to find the ways into the general ledger.

Later during the marketing execution and automation, the programs can then be used as central anchors for the agile campaign interactions and return on marketing investment calculations. While the program is part of the budgeting process, it is the underlying campaigns and activations that follow the freedom of reallocation of activation costs based on the most performing channel mix and creative assets. In most cases I've seen in the last few years, the marketing planning that is based on programs, media-types, etc. needs to fit the constraints set by the CFO and his team on an aggregated top-down monthly level. In reality, 99% of the cases don't fit the needs of the CMO and his marketing department. The multi-layered approach of top-down budgeting on programs, based on intelligent algorithms and standard finance processes with the agility of a campaign and A/B driven bottom-up marketing campaign process, looks like the winning set up of modern days.

Impact

- By synchronizing the marketing and finance world with ongoing work and a lot of effort, you can maintain the budget on different levels with program/campaign planned costs eliminated. This time can be used to focus on the real world by optimizing the activations in massive A/B testings, your marketing gets more effective.
- The clear 1:1 relationship between marketing programs and general ledger line items allows us to assign other cost types like production costs later in the process to the overall marketing spending to get a full return on marketing investment overview and a comprehensive realistic view on your marketing success.

Fields of Actions

- Design and establish a 1:1 relationship between the finance world (general/sub-ledger line items) and the marketing universe (program level).
- Design and establish clear monthly and yearly closure activities.
- Check and manage all finance exception like yearly spill-overs, accruals, barter deals, etc.
- Design and establish intelligent algorithms to derive necessary budgets out of data gained in the past and the goal definitions of a marketing program.

IT Support and Platforms

- ERP — Finance and Controlling.
- APIs to sync the finance and marketing clouds.

M3.3 Plan Alignment, Innovation, and Collaboration

As said in my previous chapter about physical laws and marketing, the light speed of marketing is creativity. Even if data could change the gravity grid of our universe, we will not attract people with boring activation and messages. For that reason, we must think about the enhancement of our strict marketing planning in form of portfolios, plans, programs, campaigns, and activations.

What we need is a more collaborative way of interacting on top of our strict planning and revision cycles. Globally executed data-driven marketing plans are no longer dubbed a one-man show where masterminds and/or agencies take over the responsibility to run independently the full programs.

Instead, each program is a carefully balanced mix of paid, owned, and earned campaigns and activations that need to be aligned centrally at the beginning of each planning period. Regular communication to the participating teams during this is key so you can keep everybody up-to-date rapidly. It helps to include the traditional marketing capabilities of creativity and innovation besides the pure budgeting and KPI planning.

The filigree balance between the centrally controlled or supervised marketing with distributed automation and the execution needs to be set up and based on a collaborative process and platform. Beginning with strategic keynotes that inform all involved parties about the overall direction and goals ongoing feedback, rating, and approval process is best because it shows the way of control a CMO foresees for his marketing universe.

Impact

- A well-balanced marketing message across all media channels and customer touchpoints are more than the sum of each activation — the conversion through your funnel will increase significantly.
- Collaboration stimulates creativity, which is the easy way of sharing new ideas, actively inform groups via push posts and pull posts, and share information across management and topic blogs enables the full swarm intelligence of your marketing universe.
- The data-driven decision should not eliminate the core success factors of marketing — innovation and creativity — as light speed in marketing is still a creative way of reaching the attention of your strategic audience.

Fields of Actions

- Design and establish the data-driven processes, platforms, and organizations so they stimulate creativity and innovation.
- Establish collaboration between all parties involved in the paid, owned, and earned activations and the customer journey.
- Start your planning cycles with a strategic key-note from the CMO.

IT Support and Platforms

- Collaboration platforms.
- Workflow systems.
- Feedback and survey systems.

M4 CREATIVE MANAGEMENT

To follow our paradigm of intelligent data-driven marketing there are three main ingredients for a winning marketing machine: data, budget, and creativity.

Now, it's time to look more in-depth at the way we enable creativity, manage the demand and production of our creative assets, and how to optimize them during the execution of our campaigns.

For me, this section of the book includes two of the most exciting topics in the marketing universe: the creative demand process and the dynamic content optimization piece.

Designing and establishing a demand and production process is key; it has also been extremely eye-opening in each marketing transformation I've been involved in. Once, I was requested to transform the marketing department of a consulting company. The more than 10,000 employees were very proud of the way they published thought leadership via their webpage and social canvas. This was done by the different service lines; in total, the firm had more than 600 different teams providing all kinds of services to the market. Before we established central marketing planning, all of those teams individually pushed their campaigns to the market; this was a quite opportunistic and locally executed campaign setup, but once we had a common plan in place with multiple programs covering all their go-to-market topics and filled them up with campaigns and activations, they realized two things: there is never enough budget to include all the topics into the market and even in the unlikely event that it was possible, there's no way such a huge amount of marketing assets for all customer touch-points could be created. The lesson was crystal clear: everybody likes to present at the market. It's easy to plan something, but it's quite different to deliver all the creative work that you had planned and for it to provide a comprehensive media and creative asset package to push this to the market.

Another good example of content production I've seen is by a consumer goods client, which was one of the biggest social brands in the world. We were involved in several analytics projects and one has dealt with their social media channels, namely Facebook. We came up with ideas for more than 1000 posts a day! This means to keep the pace, they had to post content approximately every minute. Just imagine, this means for every post, there were a few paragraphs of text, hashtags, and an image or graphic. This was all innovated, produced, polished, and approved! Now, let's have a look at the ma.tomics dealing with the way we find creative ways to gain attention and for the underlying process of demand and production of creative assets.

M4.1 Creative Ideation — Design Thinking

I'm deeply convinced that the intellectual virtue of the good old mad-men area of "creativity" is still a winning factor in today's marketing world. To gain the attention of the preferred target audiences apart from using data, you should use creative ways to communicate, and having outstanding marketing assets is a must. This means for today's marketeer, one of the goals they have aside from the standard showing return on marketing investments is to always be surprising by staying in line with the brand roots and equity. It is one of the main reasons why we still see different types of employees in the finance and marketing team — even if both are dealing with numbers.

As creative people like to work in a creative space, no wonder the new Standford D-School approaches of design thinking are now also used to develop new ways of communication.

These modern ideation processes support the birth of something new by simultaneously receiving early feedback from the customers on what works and what needs to be improved. It is not only the ideation for new creatives but also the way to interact with the customers (experimental marketing) that needs to be considered for the successful implementation of new and innovative customer journeys. While creative ideation focuses on the topic of generating new innovative content and formats, the optimization masters the ongoing A/B testing of the originally identified hero creatives and assets.

One of the most interesting parts I've seen over the last few years is that these new formats can be further customized in real-time via new technology platforms. This real-time personalization of the formally static creative assets helps to perfectly undermine the desired call-to-action with an emotional customer sense by delivering the most efficient messages, designs, and sounds based on the desired target audience.

This means creative ideation needs to focus on three topics: first the creative asset itself: second, the way of communication and how they leverage the assets: third, the technical possibilities to optimize channel and asset by real-time personalization.

Impact

- Creativity is key for awareness, which means high awareness in the upper funnel is the basement for finally converting the customers within lower funnel layers.
- New ways of customer activation and journeys in form of experimental marketing generates high attention and a broader reach to audiences you might not be able to target via your classical marketing channels.
- New ways and journeys to get in contact with selected target audiences in form of experiential marketing generate high attention.

Fields of Actions

- Enable the organization to use design thinking frameworks to create new ways of communication.
- Establish a process within your campaign planning to leverage the new ideation skills within each campaign.

IT Support and Platforms

- Collaboration platforms and (virtual) whiteboards.
- Design thinking platforms.
- Workflow systems.

M4.2 Creative Development and Delivery

While the former ma.tomic deals heavily with creativity, this is the more formal and controlled management of all types of creative assets. Even in our connected world, I've seen quite a few clients sharing their assets via local drives, USB hard disks, and e-mail.

State of the art marketing asset management is far beyond the mere storing and accessing of banners and movies and document management systems. It starts with a clear demand for creative assets and formats; it also includes the production and enterprise-wide approval, thus a collaborative workflow is a key for this, as well as the storing and sharing functionalities.

On-time deliveries of all relevant creatives and content for the full range of marketing programs need to be seamlessly integrated into the campaign preparation. This doesn't sound that complex but there is a huge variety in formats, which sometimes consumes hundreds of gigabytes, blocks huge drive space, and still opens challenges moving these files rapidly around the world.

While most of the CMOs I've consulted classified digital asset management clouds as necessary but also as a cost block, there was a view who also treated these platforms to generate a competitive advantage. Tagging your assets means also building a data repository so you can always find the best fitting image and movie for your target audience. One of my clients, who was famous for his storytelling approach in marketing, had millions of static and moving images. While in the first phase, he only focused on the pure management of these assets, in the second one, he was only handling the tagging. A real cohort of students worked for several weeks to tag every scene of all movies — they used hundreds of tags. Furthermore, AI helped to tag the scenes by providing additional tags automatically. The result was impressive; the search for new assets allowed me to search for things like this: "I need a movie where a sporty woman with sunglasses is sitting somewhere in mountains to later use her mountain bike to show a cool downhill adventure."

Another client went even further than this, which was rather impressive, and added some kind of real-time repository to his digital asset management system. A real-time crawler checked famous networks and sites through image and tag recognition. The campaign team was alerted and by this and they could then include movies people added to the social networks in realtime into their campaigns. This is a real competitive advantage!

Impact

- A globally organized and aligned creative demand management guarantees a consistent brand message and allows to centralize the content production.
- On-time delivery of creative assets help to prepare and execute the campaigns in an agile way and avoid time-consuming back and forth emails within the campaign preparation phase.
- Tagged marketing assets build a competitive advantage for search and are the fundamental base to build highly sophisticated and predictive models for user journey analysis and predictive models.

Fields of Actions

- Design and establish a global content taxonomy and tagging process.
- Integrate the creative demand and production within the marketing planning and campaign preparation processes.
- Implement rollout and enable a digital asset management cloud.

IT Support and Platforms

- Digital asset management cloud.
- Tagging system and taxonomy (master data management).
- AI tagging, image recognition, and searches.

M4.3 Creative Optimization

As of now, we have been exposed to two ma.tomics that deal with the ideation for new creative assets and ways of communication, and other ways we tag and manage the assets. The last one in this section is the art of integration into your campaign execution.

While creative ideation focuses on the topic of generating new innovative content and formats, optimization masters the ongoing A/B testing of the originally identified hero creatives and assets.

Real-time personalization of creative assets helps to perfectly undermine the desired call-to-action with emotion by delivering the most efficient messages, designs, and sounds.

This ma.tomic enables you to use your collected first-party data and external data to leverage the taxonomy and tagging efforts you invested in the former ma.tomic of creative development and delivery. Your target groups can easily cluster, so to find the most efficient creative, you must do a lot of A/B testing as well as employ more sophisticated algorithms.

So how does this work? Well, let me introduce, yet again, one of my favorite cases I've seen before. So, there was a huge car manufacturer that installed in the upper funnel a data management platform to capture the web behavior of his prospects and future customers. During the web-configuration, there were four essential attributes: the car model, the color, the type of wheels, and the interior; they were tracked thoroughly against every visitor of the configurator. The retargeting engine was able to advertise to these audiences with personalized digital banners and videos. Instead of using generic advertising assets, the customer rendered 100% personalized creatives, showing the exact car model the prospects configured with their previous web visits. The conversion rate of this kind of asset was far beyond the one we have seen before introducing this art of creative optimization.

Impact

- A permanent optimization toward the best performing creatives based on the message, the format, the sound, and colors will increase the conversion rates.
- Insights generated out of multiple tests will help to design high performing and viral marketing assets.
- Behavioral data in combination with your tagged assets will help to identify best working creative assets and by that help to eliminate production costs (waste) for non-working ones.

Fields of Actions

- Establish an ongoing optimization cycle within the campaign execution for identifying the best creatives.
- Implement an AI-based algorithm to calculate and predict the best working assets to generate top-performing conversions.

IT Support and Platforms

- Data management platform integrations.
- A/B testing and personalization engines.
- AI recommendations.

M5 AGILE CAMPAIGNS MANAGEMENT

Ma.tomics is the opportunity to set up your new math-man marketing by combining more than 50 isolated atoms to form a comprehensive solid-state block of competitive advantage. However, ma.tomics also includes ma.tom which can be seen as an abbreviation of "marketing — agile target operating model." It's now time to bring in this new iterative way of executing and implementing projects. The program Agile has its roots in software development (Scrum and DevOps) and the production of goods (lean, kanban).

I was allowed to participate in one of the training sessions from the inventor of Scrum, Jeff Sutherland, to gain my scrum master. While most people focus more on using Agile and Scrum within the world of software development, I was thrilled at the idea of bringing it into the world of marketing. To veer away from the good old mad-men waterfall style of starting with creativity to rush the planning of a complete campaign, you should ask for the budget, execute this, and hope there will be an increase in awareness and sales. What about installing a target operating model that allows you to learn during execution how to get better every single day and sprint?

For most of my clients, Agile is an essential pillar in the transformation towards an intelligent way of executing data-driven marketing. The idea of splitting your campaign execution into tiny sprints of one or two weeks, build interdisciplinary and channel overarching teams, and acting together on a simple set of rules is going to drive your return on marketing investment into new hemispheres. This is also the reason why Jeff's book about doing twice as much in half of the time (Sutherland, 2014) is a mandatory section in every one of my training sessions on intelligent data-driven marketing. Therefore, now comes a full set of good reasons to dig more into this topic and learn about the ma.tomics dealing with agile campaign management.

M5.1 Be Fast and Flexible: Campaign Preparation

While strategic marketing planning enables us to structure the planning period in a strict top-down approach, the preparation and execution of those campaigns need to be more flexible. Often I'm comparing these two sets of processes working in opposite directions with a chess field. Strategic planning builds the field of action and defines the set of tiles you'd to act on. Here, we are talking about an overall goal, budget, strategic audiences, and communication strategy. An Agile campaign is the new way of preparation and execution; this means acting in one single tile of the chessboard within the constraints set during marketing planning but it has the freedom to customize the details to the insights all the data will give you every day. This means once you've stepped out of the planning cycle, the Agile way of things will help to find and ongoing optimize the best mix of paid, owned and earned activations to push the desired message into the market.

Agile campaign preparation and execution allow us to adapt our route into the market in short sprints and to react flexibly based on the customer's behavior and feedback. Besides this way of preparing and executing push campaigns, there is also the intelligent design and optimization of the complex user journey (pull campaigns) that need to be incorporated into the overall marketing planning. This will be covered further down the road in another section. This ma.tomic deals with the new options of increased flexibility and speed of adopting the campaign to the requirements of your audience for maximum conversions.

Impact

- While the overall program planning will define some kind of grid of constraints, we are allowed to prepare the campaigns. The Agile preparation takes advantage of the flexibility to adapt the marketing execution to the best way to touch base with the customers, which increases conversions and lowers the cost per action.
- By planning less in the beginning and define the way to design the journeys and campaigns while running instead, will then cut out the time-consuming and needless pieces in the planning process — which saves money.
- By building agile swot teams for each campaign, the responsibility is moved from the top to the bottom of your organization. Studies show people are more efficient working in these setups and they spend more time on their daily tasks and are more enthusiastic about them.
- Efforts for the yearly planning cycle will be massively reduced and can be moved toward more creative thinking and ideation which will end-up in higher conversions and sales.

Fields of Actions

- Establish an Agile campaign and prepare the journey process within the organization, including new roles and responsibilities.
- Train your organization to think and act with agility in mind.
- Roll out a platform that provides a holistic overview of each planned paid, owned, and earned activation within a single plan.
- Plan consequent A/B testing and execution within sprints for all campaigns and activations, and provide the results to your teams to consequently adapt the campaign to market needs.

IT Support and Platforms

- Agile campaign planning system.
- Marketing automation clouds, including the customer journeys and segmentation.
- A/B testing modules.
- Workflow systems for content and campaigns.
- Data and analytics clouds, for example, paid, owned, earned campaign dashboards.

M5.2 Run Fast, Fail Fast: Campaign Execution

Execution of campaigns and journeys is the final moment of truth — when the strategic planning and Agile preparation hits the market, your prospects, and customers. While in the previous section, there was discussion about the ma.tomics that are about flexibility and speed to market the execution piece, this section refers to your organization's capability to run fast and fail fast. An integration and collaborative management of all players being a part of the execution is key to be successful. To master this, all customer-facing teams such as agencies, owned communication channels, event management, consumer activation teams, sales teams, etc. need to work closely together to provide the perfect customer experience. As mentioned above, all of them attempt to learn from the past data gathered in previous sprints and avoid pointing the finger at others because of any failures they made in the past.

Most people are aware of a short story about a math professor who started scribbling on his chalkboard with the multiplication table for the number

9. 1 times 9 is nine, 2 times 9 is 18, 3 times 9 is 27, and so on. Finally on the last line, 10 times 9, he writes 91 instead of 90. Immediately the class, who were paying attention, give him grief for writing the wrong number. His reply to them was simple, yet mind-blowing. He said, "Dear students, I've done nine sums correct; I only failed once!" So, run fast, fail fast means to deliberately run into situations where you might lose money or where the approach isn't perfect. On the other hand, as long as this isn't the full campaign and you can identify the underlying issue and how to solve it, then next time you will do it better. So, next time you have your daily stand-up with the team or the campaign retrospective meeting at the end of the sprint (a sprint is a week), this means you will get better every day during your campaign execution.

To summarize, the Agile principle in the ma.tomic here — "run fast, fail fast" means enabling the organization to work in short iterations to allow huge, ongoing A/B Testing and learn from what runs well and learn even more from the things you have messed up.

Impact

- Run fast, fail fast approaches flip the current approach of running campaigns and journeys in a waterfall model. Failures are explicitly allowed and also intrinsically integrated into the execution to learn from it and to improve so you obtain better conversions, cost per actions, and more sales revenue.
- KPI systems and feedback cycles are more open and balanced; the customer and his perfect experience will be put in the middle of every day's work to increase customer experience and loyalty — the customer lifetime value and net promotor score will increase.

Fields of Actions

- Establish a culture of learning from failure instead of appraising only success.
- Enable and train your organization to think and act in agile ways.
- Change the KPI system towards a "learning" ecosystem.
- Establish ongoing A/B testing and experiments within each campaign and journey.

IT Support and Platforms

- Agile campaign planning system.
- Marketing automation clouds, including customer journeys and segmentation.
- A/B testing modules.
- Workflow systems for content and campaigns.
- Data and analytics clouds, for example, paid, owned, and earned campaign dashboards.

M5.3 Manage Trigger-Based Campaigns: Campaign Automation

The campaign preparation and execution phase is split into two slightly different approaches. There is the classic way of pushing campaigns into the market and on the other side, there is the possibility to involve the customers through triggers into several customer journeys without any active user activation via pushed activations.

This second way of executing pull campaigns that are based on marketing automation is becoming more popular. With the early advent of marketing automation software, we all had this dream of setting up the journeys, sitting back, and letting the machine do the work. The only thing left open was to count the endless amount of money you'd earn with your perfect user journeys. We all learned the hard way that this was merely the dream of the marketing cloud provider. The reality was that their extremely expensive clouds used certain triggers to generate a mass of emails that pestered the customers instead of increasing the conversion rates. Step by step, the leaders outpaced the laggards by learning how to leverage this automation by only focusing on certain parts of the funnel and the best working triggers. The need for regular cleaning activities arrived and was also part of maintaining your competitive advantage.

I've seen a lot of clients that leveraged the easy way of adding customer journeys; the culture of fail fast and the exploding number of channels reaching out to the customers. Where they ended up was not what they expected! A huge bunch of customer journeys running wild in pushing out emails, text messages, and other customer activations. To stay on top of this, it is key to control the customer experience and maintain your journey portfolio. For this reason, clear governance needs to be in place ascertaining who is allowed to add and change customer journeys. This is nothing else than designing the best working customer experience in an agile way, similarly to the previous two ma.tomics.

Impact

- Campaign automation enables you to serve the customers in a personalized way without the investment into headcounts to push our activations.
- Customers can be involved in several journeys to satisfy different needs at the same time without doubling the costs.
- The integration of AI into the campaign automation opens new machine-based insights within customer segmentation, personalization of the content, and product recommendations that will affect your conversions and cost per action.
- Without a proper and fully rolled-out governance model, there is the risk of running against privacy constraints and also violating the customer relationship.

Fields of Actions

- Design and rollout campaign automation platforms within the marketing technology stack.
- Evolve from pure push campaigns towards the use of journeys within the marketing department.
- Establish and activate clear governance and RACI matrix within the marketing organization.
- Integrate the journey concept into the overall strategic planning approach.

IT Support and Platforms

- Marketing automation clouds, including customer journeys and segmentation.
- A/B Testing, personalization, and recommendation modules.
- Approvals and workflow for journey maintenance.

M6 PROFILING — KNOWN & UNKNOWN AUDIENCES

With the group of profiling ma.tomics, we leave behind the world of pure planning, creative production, and campaign execution to lay down the fundament for a real customer-centric and data-driven marketing ecosystem. Companies who like to climb the maturity curve from mad-men marketing towards an audience-driven math-men need to pay extra attention to these ma.tomics. Big data profiles allow you to store besides the demographic and transactional data a myriad of behavioral data. Therefore, they are the perfect base for later manual and artificial segmentation, scorings and by that essential for all personalizations and recommendations used in the ma.tomic of paid, owned, and earned activations. Here, in this section, we need to tackle the topic of what is legally allowed and what is legitimate from the point of view of a prospect and customer.

M6.1 The golden record of your customers

In the previous days of marketing, the context where marketeers assumed to meet their customers and prospects led most of the decisions. For the new sporty running shoes, the CMO decided to go for cinema pre-rolls in an adventure movie and a mid-roll in the famous "how to run a marathon" podcast. On top, some display ads in the new training app should help him meet the sporty people he'd like to reach. What he was not aware of was that most of his shoes were bought by parents for their children as the shows drew away from sporty running equipment towards a "must-have" and cool sneaker for hip youngsters.

The modern CMO now knows his prospects and customers. From the first touchpoint on the webpage or in the running app, he uses a system and a unique identifier that builds the central anchor to multiple further IDs. This can be cookies, mobile IDs, emails, phone numbers, logins, etc. Whether it's in a B2B or B2C model, the ultimate goal is to know the audience in person by their unique IDs (known-unknown, e.g. cookies) and personalized identifiers (known-known, e.g. e-mail address). Based on both data pools, marketers will be able to consolidate all the information in a golden record of a single profile. To allow cross-system analytics an enterprise-wide taxonomy does help to establish the canonical data model. This model is used by AI algorithms and the intelligent graph data structures will help to collect complex network structures to merge and split profiles that are collected via millions of different sessions (see also ma.tomic: M12 Cross-device and platform).

Today, this fully audience-centric approach allows us to directly touch-base with the customers. All interactions are logged in a canonical data model to build comprehensive 360° customer profiles. These profiles are used for analytics on real behavioral interactions. The data is replacing gut feelings and your segmentation will hit the most performing audiences. This helps segmentation for retargeting campaigns, look-a-like modeling, personalization, and recommendations will be implemented on real profiles and insights instead of the assumption to meet somebody somewhere as the context looks promising.

Impact

- A comprehensive 360° customer record including all master and transactional data is the starting point of each audience-centric marketing activity; it replaces gut feelings with data-driven decisions that normally show much higher conversions and lower cost per action.
- The golden record allows a fine granular segmentation to run the best performing personalization and recommendations to avoid inefficiencies in your campaigns and customer interactions.
- To run AI-based cluster analysis and regressions to harvest the rich golden record is a pre-requisite.

Fields of Actions

- Build out a clear taxonomy of a golden record (see ma.tomic M2.2) to establish a canonical data model and cube.
- Design and carry a DMP (Data Management Platform) and CDP (Customer Data Platform) that collects all of your first-party data on all owned properties and channels.
- Connect the DMP and CDP to your segmentation engine and customer journeys to take advantage of programmatic buying platforms (retargeting) and personalized customer touchpoints (onsite personalization and recommendation).
- Guarantee the need to be compliant with data protection rules and constraints.

IT Support and Platforms

- Customer 360° Profile Platform (DMP and CDP).
- Segmentation engine.
- Connector to the different customer journeys.
- Real-time Interaction monitoring (behavioral tracking).

M6.2 The "Known-Unknown" Asset of Audience Data

Even if modern marketing literature is always talking about experience, customer journeys, etc. I'm still a fan of the good old marketing funnel. First, you should generate awareness by attracting the interest of your prospects. Try to influence them so they desire your new product, and give them the option to act and acquire the product. While the sales departments realized early on that they should know their customers for further up and cross-selling, the marketers often claimed that they couldn't identify the people in this upper awareness and interest funnel. However, in our digital and data-driven world, this is no longer true. From the first interaction with the brand, there is a way to follow your prospects down the funnel to the final purchase decision. Whether this is based on cookies, fingerprints, logins, etc. — I'm 100% convinced money follows eyeballs and thus there will be always ways to track your prospects. Besides the well-established CRM customer records and real identifiers like e-mail, etc. there is a world of know-unknown prospects that help you take advantage of the same algorithms, analytics, and segmentations that are used in the known-known world. This means modern marketing is built upon two central databases: a data management platform (DMP) for anonymization and a customer database (CDP) for all personalized data. In the past, classic CRM application profiles were based on only a few, fundamental personalized data like addresses and a few marketing attributes (e.g. likes sports). The digital world allows companies to start much earlier in the customer journey and collect richer and broader insights based on the (browsing) behavior of the prospects. Through cookies, mobile identifiers, and fingerprints, a known-unknown profile is possible within a data management platform.

It is used as the starting point to track each single user journey in a digital world; it can be used to run high performing retargeting campaigns and to control sophisticated user journeys without the need to know who is behind these transactions — as aforementioned, this ma.tomic "profiling" is dealing with a know-unknown profile asset.

Impact

- Starting much earlier, tracking the known-unknown prospects and customers allows companies to run personalized messages and recommendations within the user journey resulting in higher conversions.

- The huge amount of millions of data-points collected against cookies, hashed emails, logins, mobile-IDs, etc. is the pre-requisite to run sophisticated browsing analysis in the upper marketing funnel and to increase the conversion toward desire and action.
- By collection impressions, the known-unknown data pool is also the basis for marketing mix modeling and attribution model analysis to optimize the marketing spends.

Fields of Actions

- Design and roll out a data management platform.
- Manage the change to start tracking user behavior much earlier in the marketing funnel/journey.

IT Support and Platforms

- DMP — data management platform.
- CDP — Customer Database Platform

M6.3 Fundamental base work — Content Tagging

This part isn't as complex as it may seem; the previous two ma.tomics get you to establish two interconnected profiles to track the full marketing funnel from awareness down to the final actions. However, once you dig deeper, it shows what behavioral tracking means. We are talking about a machine and data lake that can store millions and billions of data points. But the content and value of each point need to be defined. Here is a short view of the most classical case of tracking user behavior on a webpage. The data shows the user-ID was on page ABC. He scrolled down 50% of the page and has spent 48 seconds there before he left to open page XYZ. Hmm ... as long as we do not know what was on page ABC and XYZ or precisely what was in the middle of ABC where he has spent 48 seconds, the information is worthless. This means apart from profiling already known customers or unknown-known prospects, without a proper tagging of marketing assets and owned content this does not work.

All the owned content and paid marketing assets need to be tagged with the correct information based on an enterprise-wide synchronized and used content taxonomy. Only by doing this, it will be possible to analyze where people are interested and what are the most performing topics within the marketing ecosystem. This is done in one of two ways: the boring and time-consuming way which is the better quality one is to use humans to adds tags to each side, app, creative, etc. used in customer interaction. What has helped over the last few years is machine learning, computation power, highly sophisticated algorithms, and crawlers replacing the human brain by tagging sites, videos, and assets automatically.

Impact

- A comprehensive content taxonomy implemented on all the used marketing assets allows companies to collect the rich first-party data lake that is used within customer profiling and segmentation. Time-consuming consolidation and merging of different data structures are no longer necessary.

Fields of Actions

- Design and roll out a content taxonomy.
- Design and roll out a tagging solution.
- Establish a clear master data management solution for ongoing updates of the content tagging.

IT Support and Platforms

- Tagging solution.
- Master data management and governance solution.
- Automatic crawler and tagging algorithms.

M6.4 Consent Management — Customer Buy-In

Just imagine how you think, feel and behave in the real world. Somebody who takes a drink at a bar with his best friend is aware that the barkeeper may hear parts of the stories they are telling. Therefore, that person acknowledges there is a third-party involved and that third-party may spread their stories and tell them to others. If you visit a doctor or lawyer, you naturally rely on the fact that these groups of people will not spread any information about you to any third party. The good thing this is also written worldwide into several laws. In the early mad-men days, nobody expected that there will be a time where the same laws will be necessary and implemented for marketing data. As we have seen in the previous three ma.tomics modern marketing profiles are built out of thousands of attributes that allow companies to draw up a realistic, comprehensive picture of the real person behind the tracked ID.

Thus, the advent of general data protection rules was so obvious and necessary, and they have to follow the same rules we have in the real world. We enter an environment like a bar, the doctor's room, a layers office, etc., and expect certain rules. Often, if we are not sure how these rules are set, we wish for a short pre-alignment of how this will happen. In the world of marketing, this is consent; it is the central alignment between me as a prospect or customer and the advertiser as to how he will the collected data during the next interaction. Nowadays, people are expected to manage their digital user consent and data in a centralized profile with each organization they interact with. Here they can change their master data (e.g. bank account, email), see their behavioral data and define how the data can be used inside and possibly outside of the enterprise.

In many large parts of the world, strict privacy rules even enforce us to provide this central access to all user data. On top of this, we as a host of the data collection, need to provide the ability to download all customer data, stop the processing of the data and finally enforce the full deletion of all the profile data (e.g. GDPR within the European Union). Therefore marketing without consent management no longer works. The user consent defines how people like to be involved in any communication. User consent needs to be an intrinsic piece of every customer 360° profile management and every user interaction needs to take care of what was the explicit definition of how to be treated the user once has given.

Impact

- Without consistent consent management, there is a high risk of violating local privacy laws. This may end up in huge financial penalties.
- Consent management gives the user the possibility to precisely define the ways they like to be contacted and advertised by the company — this helps to increase customer satisfaction and loyalty.

Fields of Actions

- Install a central data protection team and train all involved parties on the importance of the legal and legitimate way of working with customer data.

- Implement central consent management within your customer data platform and connect all activation platforms. Be sure that a historical archive of the terms and conditions allows you to show the type of consent your counterparts have agreed on.
- Install comprehensive documentation and legal workflow for working with customer data.
- Implement one central profile access for all known customers and prospects, where they can easily access their data, ask for it to be deleted, or change it, or put it on hold.

IT Support and Platforms

- Consent management platforms and user access profiles, including a historic archive with the terms and conditions you have and are aligned with your customers and prospects.
- Reporting and governance platforms to document how data is processed.

M6.5 Data Protection — Legal and Legitimate

Many of us have seen this paradigm several times: "Data is the new oil." Data is a corporate-wide asset that finds its way into the balance sheet of enterprises. I have not seen any company in the last five years that are not thinking about how to leverage the data they gather within their specific business model. We have also seen innovations like the digital twins of different, real entities we see in the business world — whether this is a customer, a product, or a service. As a trade-off, this immense appetite for data includes a huge portion of financial and brand value risk. In our previous ma.tomic, it was demonstrated that without proper consent management and treating customer data illegally, we face the threat of huge financial penalties that may cover up to 4% of the global net revenues of the company.

The strong alignment with local data protection rules (e.g. GDPR in the European Union) and the risk of mitigation strategies in case of data breaches and negative press releases that are blamed on a data octopus is an essential part of each data-driven marketing implementation. However, is this the only thing you need to pay attention to? With the right consent, you're more or less allowed to process the customer data however you like. No law in the world does not allow the retargeting itself or the possibility of selling this data. The only crucial thing is to be in line with the law and ask for the right consent. Let's go back to our doctor's example from the previous chapter. Just imagine you would have signed a 200-page document up-front, where you agree on page 130 on the bottom in a three-line cryptic paragraph that the doctor is allowed to share your health files. At the moment you realize, that your employer, your friends, and maybe also your opponents now know all about your current health, you would start suing your doctor. He would come back with the signed contract, explaining to you that he's in line with current law. What will happen after that is you won't visit this doctor ever again. You'd also ensure that your family and friends knew about the situation so they too, didn't visit this specific doctor.

The same happens in marketing, though not in the black and white shape I've explained. People feel that this advertiser is using their data very aggressively at the edge of what is allowed. We have all seen the lawsuits and GOP hearings in the US against the big silicon valley internet companies. Thus, every CMO needs to carefully balance the value of data with the feelings of customers and what is legitimately related to profiling and retargeting. Intelligent data-driven marketing is set up for this reason; it always has customer satisfaction and happiness, brand value, and the sentiment and share of voice as a central KPI in the frequent feedback loops.

Impact

- Besides the thread of high financial penalties, the damage in brand value can push your company into an uncomfortable position. Shit storms and brand damage can cause also massive financial losses.
- The open and transparent way of how you use the customer data, what benefits they will gain (better recommendations, faster transactions, etc.) helps to increase the trust in your brands. This means switching barriers rise and customers convert more easily to real fans and ambassadors.

Fields of Actions

- Align with all local data privacy rules and implement necessary actions (e.g. cookie banners, profile centers, ...) as well as a way your prospects and customer can understand how you like to use their data and for the reasons you like to collect the data points.

- Define a clear communication plan and emergency guide for all kinds of possible data breaches and issues.
- Design and implement a strict data access "roles and rights" policy.
- Design and implement regular data protection and security audits.

IT Support and Platforms

- Terms and conditions, consent management platforms, and user access profiles, including a historic archive on the terms and conditions you have that align with your customers and prospects.
- Include the data access model into your master data management and governance.
- Reporting and governance platforms for documenting how the data is processed.

M7 HYPER ACCURATE TARGETING and LOOK-A-LIKE

As introduced in the previous ma.tomic group the big data profiles of modern math-men marketing build the essential core of the hyper-accurate targeting possibility. Two challenges need to be overcome in this field of action. First, the translation from the strategic audience toward a tactical segment that can be reached in a digital world and on every touch-point. Second, the paradox with the better ways of building hyper-accurate targets, the reach within each segment decreases significantly. I've seen a lot of clients run into this trap. Whenever I've seen shiny slides with incredible increases in click-through rates, unbelievable CPAs, and conversions, my first reaction has been to challenge the drafter with the question about the reach and share on the total audience. Remember our frame of reference in the second Gedankenexperiment; even if the set of measures is a small number of values, you should always have these in focus to get a full picture of your marketing universe. Most of the time, these fantastic figures were reached on a tiny segment of few people and not on the broad scale of your total addressable audience. The look-a-like is a perfect ma.tomic to escape from this paradox, find the reach, and secure the high conversion rates.

M7.1 Plan & Design — Strategic Audiences

While the ma.tomic of the "marketing universe" defines the overall goals within related strategic customer and market access strategies, it's time to think about strategic audiences and how to reach them with your marketing programs. This means our overall definition of whom we'd like to reach needs to be translated into a real way of accessing these segments within our marketing universe.

It's where we close the loop, based on the insights we gained in the data and analytics domain; a new round of planning needs to take care of this and start thinking about allocating budget to the most promising audiences. We might see in our data, that young and hip people are less represented in our current reach, thus we might start planning to address more of them in the next round. However, fewer people does not automatically mean a segment with higher potential. The product just may not be attractive and for that reason, we see less of them in our marketing universe. Thus, we might like to define the new strategic audience "Gen Z in Country ABC" as a valid try for one or two of our future marketing programs. The strategic audience may be defined based on the owned data pools but also the access to publicly available data pools that help to identify the most promising audiences for the programs. These strategic audiences are also the fundamental base to estimate the maximum and realistic reach and frequency caps within the different marketing channels.

Based on this 30,000 ft planning, we're now able to dive deeper into the design of our marketing campaigns by translating our overarching goals and strategic audiences into target audiences we like to address in our journeys and campaigns. This means we are moving away from pure planning exercises toward the concrete design of our customer activations. I've seen this several times; there was no seamless way from the initial planning towards the real activation of audiences. People are always thinking they act customer-centric and audience-driven but in the end, this is more a theoretical endeavor instead of a real breakdown from high-level audiences towards tactical segments (see next ma.tomic "Build & Activate — Tactical Segments"). You're asking yourself: what should this look like? Just think about these endless attempts to design an experience based on personas and use-cases. I'm not sure when I've seen this first, but during the hype cycle beginning of this century, there was not a single marketing workshop not claiming that personas are the golden egg of endless riches and the beginning of 100% predictable customer behavior. As time goes on, we've seen that this isn't true and there's a huge gap between experience design based on personas and the experience implementation later in the "real marketing universe."

I remember one customer who reached out to me with an extremely shiny presentation of his new strategic audiences. The main people they needed to look at were "silver singles" and "wealthy couples." The slides and definitions of these two audiences looked quite nice, however, the problem was that the client couldn't distinguish both of them within his audiences. They acted the same in their online behavior and the first-party data pool was that poor that all the money for the persona design has not helped to define more accurate targets. Thus, whenever you start thinking about the planning for new strategic audiences, ensure you also include the step of translating them within your specific marketing universe into target audiences.

Impact

- Strategic audiences help to stay focused and in case you can address them later in your universe to deliver the right message to the right audience.

- Success KPIs can be bound to strategic audiences to identify the most effective target groups to ongoing use these insights within your closed-loop marketing cycles.
- The definition of strategic audiences allows consistent talk to the target groups independent from the used media channel (classic, digital, field, and sales force, etc.), and by doing that, you can reach higher conversions with these different groups of people.

Fields of Actions

- Design and implement new organizational teams dealing purely with audience management (analytics, planning, optimization) based on segments instead of activation channels.
- Design and installation of a corporate-wide marketing planning system to guarantee a consistent customer experience and communication based on strategic audiences, target groups, and correlated marketing goals, assets, and messages.
- Consistent use of audience-driven analytics and profiling.

IT Support and Platforms

- Program and campaign planning platforms.
- Audience-centric data and analytics platforms.

M7.2 Build & Activate — Tactical Segments

As we have seen in the previous ma.tomic, consistent break down from initial audience planning towards specific groups is key to be very audience-driven. This does not stop at the program planning level. Within the activation of your marketing campaigns and journeys, you need to reach all these audiences on all of your customer touchpoints at any time. To do this, each strategic marketing audience and the later designed target groups finally need to be "translated" into technical segments within each media channel and customer touchpoint. While 2010 to 2020 DMPs (data management platforms) based on cookies were used to touch base with the customer on various touchpoints we see these days more and more CDPs (customer database platforms) using multiple identifiers and graph databases to orchestrate the customer channels and journey on an end-to-end scale.

In each of these platforms, marketers could define segments based on millions of behavioral, demographical, and historic transactional data all bind strongly to one or more unique identifiers (e.g. cookies, mobile IDs, hashed emails, phone numbers, etc.). The set of IDs represent the tactical segments that are used to personalize the customer experience on each touchpoint. For that reason, these profile IDs in the DMPs and CDPs guarantee to reach the tactical and strategic audiences within all the paid, owned, and earned activations you planned in your marketing universe. Again, we see the same pattern in the plan and design phase. This kind of forensic profiling based on digital (clicks, views) and context-specific (geo locations, time-windows) touchpoints need to overcome the issue that in the real world may be two completely different strategic audiences. It shows the same behavior and can't be distinguished in a digital world. However, there wasn't a single customer I've seen in the last few years who wasn't able to increase his conversions by factor 10 just by relying on first-party data tactical segments for campaign activation and user journey definitions.

Impact

- Millions of data-points and ID-Graph-Databases (DMPs, CDPs) allow the building of hyper granular target segments that are the base for a perfect orchestrated and individual customer experience. Conversions increase in addition to increased loyalty of your customers due to this consequent personalization and re-targeting.
- Automated user journeys use tactical segments as an input to provide always-on, end-to-end processes to serve your customer in the full marketing funnel.

Fields of Actions

- Design and implement a comprehensive profile graph database (CDP and DMP) with a connected segmentation engine.
- Include the use of tactical audience segments into each customer touchpoint and media channel for personalization and retargeting.

IT Support and Platforms

- Tag-management system for the data-collection and touch-point integration.
- Journey builder to design and activate always on journeys.
- Ad-tech-stack integration to sync your audiences with media activation partners.
- Real-time interaction platforms to personalize your owned activation platforms.

M7.3 Reach is King — Accurate Targets and Higher Reach

Now, we have talked a lot about strategic and tactical segments and how we can generate an impact by better personalization and recommendations based on these hyper-accurate target audiences. However, the end of your first-party data ecosystem is limited, which means even if we start to slice and dice the universe into more granular parts to gain higher conversions, the amount of customers and prospects is still the same. Only the efficiency in form of conversion rates and loyalty rates increases.

It's time to start thinking about how to overcome this dilemma of hyper granular, also super small segments with limited reach. This is the first time we need to rely on artificial intelligence and the data-driven way of working becomes true. So far, our human brain was used to build the break-down from the strategic audience toward more granular tactical audiences. We can flip this vice-versa and let a machine do this by just using the two fundamental sets of information we have in our databases. With the graph-database as the nucleus of each profile and the millions of demographic, behavioral, and transactional data, we can start using advanced clustering, regressions, and other algorithms to build our segments. The machine can calculate overlaps, similarities, etc. in the data that we as human beings are not able to see.

This is perfect; instead of doing all these brain works of slice and dice, we trust in the machine's learning power and use the segments calculated by the underlying algorithms. Still, we are limited because even the most powerful computer in the world could not increase the amount of "real" prospects and customers in our marketing universe. Really?

As you may remember, we can connect our first-party data lake toward the endless ocean of second and third-party data. With the integration into the Ad-Tech-Stack, we have direct access to millions and billions of profiles filled with thousands of attributes. The inner core of our profiles, the ID graph often is synced properly with a partner's data ecosystem and that allows direct access to their data set. Thus, our algorithms are not limited to our ecosystem; instead, we can rely on so-called look-a-like models that allow us to also consider the world-wide data ecosystem.

Modern DMP and CDP cloud platforms normally profile these connections out of the box. During several projects we used these connectors and access to run the look-a-like on billions of profiles — this is, to be honest, more or less everybody with access to the internet. As the access and the usage of second and third-party data normally costs money, the higher conversions need to be proofed against the higher costs for activation. What I've seen in many projects is that the 10 times higher conversions are still valid. A better KPI to compare the use of this data is the cost per action (CPA). Taking all tech-fees and activation costs into consideration, in most cases, there was still a factor of lower CPA for data-driven campaigns and always-on user journeys.

Impact

- The access to a nearly unlimited amount of profiles and attributes via the second and third-party data market allows us to overcome the burden of owned first-party profile access. In combination with machine learning power, look-a-like models help to build clusters with high conversion rates for first time targeting, re-targeting, and personalization.
- Additional costs for these data and profiles will be absorbed by the higher likelihood to engage with the brand and the desired actions.

Fields of Actions

- Install the correct consent within your first-party consent management to get permission to sync your profile IDs with partners and to access data pools outside your first-party data ecosystem.
- Negotiate second and third-party data partnerships.
- Technically connect and activate second and third-party data and profile access within your data management platform and customer database platform.

IT Support and Platforms

- Content management platforms.
- Data management platforms.
- Customer database platforms.
- Second and third-party data clouds.
- AI-based segmentation engines.

M8 INNOVATIVE & OPTIMIZED PEO ACTIVATION MIX

We have started with the lightweight ma.tomics and delved more into the inner core of customer-centric and data-driven math-men marketing. Now, welcome to the most important inner nucleus of our marketing universe: the paid, owned, and earned (PEO) activation mix. While most of the ma.tomics deal with general data and marketing capabilities or tasks helping to set up a highly efficient and effective marketing target operating model, this ma.tomic deals with the real customer experience and interactions. The three comprehensive clusters of paid, owned, and earned activations overarch all customer journeys and touch-points.

We will see that social and voice are often seen as an activation channel but this is not true. Both are general capabilities that need to be applied in all ma.tomics of this innovative and optimized PEO activation mix. Though, there is more to come; optimizing this mix by allocating the budget to the correct channels. The best activation still relies on the end of the price for the next action or purchase. For this reason, we also need a ma.tomic for trade promotion management, a sales-driven activation via promotions, data-driven pricing, and discounts.

M8.1 Paid (Media) Activations

Paid media advertising is still a major pillar of every marketing program. Whether these are classic channels like linear TV and radio or the world of digital touchpoints like social, display, video, and search — there are plenty of ways of reaching your audience. I've seen several clients that claimed digital paid media activation is data-driven marketing. Here I have a much broader scope in mind. For me, intelligent data-driven marketing is overarching the three major pillars of paid, owned, and earned activations with all their facilities and processes.

This ma.tomic deals with all activities around any paid activation, this includes all classic above the line channels (TV, cinema, radio, print, out of home, sponsoring, partner-events, fairs, etc.) but also the new digital channels (digital, video, search, social, influencers, etc.).

As we have learned, there are only three things we need to control on each touch-point. First, the competency to use hyper-accurate targets; second, to personalize the customer experience; and third, to give recommendations for the next best action. This sounds quite easy and logical but in all my projects, this ma.tomic and the two following with earned and owned activations has been always the most complex to analyze and implement optimizations. Just ask yourself, can I control all the touchpoints? My educated guess is that half of the readership of this book buy their paid activations via an agency without any data-sharing contract in place and technical interface. It means you're running blind; a third-party is running anything you hope this will help, to finally, once the campaign is over, show you the success on shiny powerpoints. This is something you should not accept. Furthermore, in a 100% outsourced setup, every company should be in control of which audience is activated via which channel and what were the used marketing assets to do this. Applying this ma.tomic is more than data-sharing contracts and technical interfaces to sync audiences; it is being able to personalize these channels and provide the next best actions as aforementioned.

Impact

- Paid media activation allows you to reach audiences outside of your owned ecosystem and reach people to generate awareness in the upper funnel or with the next best actions in the lower performance funnel.
- The consequent use of audience activations via re-targeting will increase the people entering your funnel, uplift the conversions, and helps to manage bounce rates in your customer journeys.

Fields of Actions

- Design and implement a well-balanced set up of in-house and agency-based paid activations processes and teams.
- Install clear data-sharing contracts and technical interfaces with your agencies.
- Guarantee to be able to personalize each touch-point and to recommend the next best actions on all paid channels.

IT Support and Platforms

- Marketing/Ad-Tech-Stack audience sync.
- Marketing planning solutions to include agencies in your campaign and journey management.

M8.2 Earned (Media) Attention

After this view on enhancing your reach via paid media activations, two ma.tomics cover the three pillars of customer interactions and user experience. The most complex field of customer activation is to design, plan, and coordinate what others talk about our brand, products, and company. There is a world where you might be able to control a well-cultivated network to press representatives, TV hosts, and other celebrities of the public show business. Even without paying for these kinds of influencers, they're able to put you in the right spotlight in case they see a benefit for their prominence. Thus, the control of earned media attention should find some attention in the strategic marketing planning, the underlying program, and campaign preparation. In a more connected world, the risk has been increasing more and more to be part of any critics being spread virally across networks and the press.

The perfect use of press-releases and content, the relationship management to publisher and alliance management to partners, the ongoing listening and management of social networks to not miss any viral effects has to be included in the daily earned activation mix.

This brings me to the second important field of action within this ma.tomic: social networks and the swarming power of millions of users via posts, likes, and shares. These users can't be controlled in the same way you treat press representatives etc. — the social clouds with all their viral network effects and shit storms behave differently. The way to survive in this jungle is to establish an operating model within your marketing department for social media listening and engagement. While most of the paid and owned activations are dealing with (triggered) push activities the earned ma.tomic includes also this pull part. Image recognition to identify brand logos, text crawler, sentiment scores, and hash-tag filters allow to stay on top of the glut that is discussed in these networks all over the world (see also next ma.tomic chapter — M9).

Let me finish this ma.tomic with one of the most discussed, prominent, and complex earned channels be it the on-site one of a search engine via search engine optimization (SEO). I've put this into the earned bucket, knowing that a big portion of my clients pays huge junks of money to special agencies to optimize their ".com" worlds. In the end, what you get back from these search engines is earned without any paid investment to the provider itself. Thus, the SEO costs should be treated in a similar way to content production costs for your storytelling in your owned ecosystem.

Impact

- Earned media attention allows you to control parts of the market to generate positive network effects. This will finally end up in higher reach and awareness.
- While a positive feedback loop may boost the reach, a shit-storm can also fully destroy brand value and sales amounts.

Fields of Actions

- Design and implement a well-balanced setup of in-house and agency-based processes, and teams to align with partners, influencers, and publishers.
- Implement an account-based relationship process and platform.
- Implement a holistic request handling process and platform.
- Implement a social listening and engagement process and platform.

IT Support and Platforms

- Social listening and engagement clouds.
- AI for image recognition and sentiment scores.
- Marketing planning solutions to include communication departments and agencies in your campaign and journey management.

M8.3 Owned Touchpoint orchestration

There is one last ma.tomic in the PEO activation mix: the owned customer experience ecosystem. While in the wild days of mad-men marketing, there were almost no ways of owned touchpoints with customers today; the world has changed fundamentally. The owned possibilities to interact with prospects and customers have emerged from events, inhouse print magazines, and rooftop logos on the firms building towards a multi-channel engagement jungle.

The dominating channel in this ma.tomic is still what we name ".com," the web and mobile company sites. Modern experience clouds allow companies to provide static content consumed via desktop, tablet, and mobile browsers.

As mentioned above, social company accounts can be used to push information in the form of posts into the different networks via a social content management system (CMS). Similar and often treated as one are owned video channels on YouTube and other portals. That's it? That's all? Sometimes it looks simple when dealing with my clients but here are plenty more ways to communicate in your owned communication. The second most prominent communication is newsletters via e-mails, followed by mobile apps, push notifications, and text messages. The next two are a bit more interactive but still owned; these are voice and chatbots. Within each organization, there is room to creatively define "new" owned channels. This could be some experiential customer touchpoints like special events or new displays provided by the internet of things devices (displays, voice).

A really big lever is your complete service and sales. Most of the CMOs do not lift this power, by including their field sales and service workforce into their campaign and journey strategies. Furthermore, your back office normally sends out hundreds of letters, emails, purchase orders, invoices, etc. per day, so just think about the right footers announcing your next hero product. Empower your workforce; if this is done right, they could generate massive reach. Just imagine six digits just by the number of people talking to their friends and followers about the latest hero product and content in different social networks and blogs — this is an enormous reach that doesn't have to be paid.

Last but not least, the guerilla teams for product and brand direct activations need to be involved and aligned within the overall channel mix. One of the fundamental questions of modern intelligent data-driven marketing is to balance, whether it might make sense to de-invest from paid campaigns to enhance the owned channel communication and customer touchpoints. The "perfect" campaign is non-paid and has the same reach to all your strategic audiences and tactical segments.

Impact

- Owned media attention allows companies to increase the reach without any further activation costs (only production costs) via web-sites, email, SMS, bots, the workforce, etc.
- The combination of paid push campaigns with owned and trigger-based customer journeys allow a 1-on-1 personalization that leads to a massive increase in customer satisfaction and conversion rates.
- Using the own workforce as a marketing channel also generates a common "we-feeling" and influence the positive communication about the brand and product.
- A streamlined control on only a few communication topics helps to stay focused and to speak as a company with one single voice.
- Experimental marketing with innovative formats takes you out of the standard marketing glut.

Fields of Actions

- Design and implement a well-balanced setup of processes and teams to include all the owned customer touchpoints into the marketing activities.
- Implement a communication platform and governance rules to control all external communication of marketing messages.
- Design and implement a balanced marketing target operating model to orchestrate all your owned and personalized customer journeys in-line with the paid campaigns.
- Install a permanent innovation cycle for experimental marketing and new formats.

IT Support and Platforms

- Experience clouds (Web/Mobile CMS).
- Social CMS.
- Video channels and CMS.
- Marketing clouds for personalized customer journeys.
- Marketing planning and resource management platforms.
- Voice and chatbot frameworks.
- Collaborative workforce communities.
- Sales clouds for workforce integration and account-based marketing.

M8.4 Social and Voice — two special capabilities

Let us have a closer look at two capabilities that can't be put into one of the paid, owned, and earned ma.tomics. I can't remember how often I have had this discussion of "where to put social" with my clients in the last years. Most people would put it below the ma.tomic of earned attention, but there are also parts in other ma.tomics like the paid and owned activations, or the chapter about viral effects.

Social can be seen in all of these buckets; there is the owned social wall that allows you to push posts through your company and employee accounts into the networks. There is a way of boosting these posts with money in the paid ma.tomic and there is the earned part when others start talking about you or share the things you've added to your social canvas. Not to mention, they can also share any experiences they've had with your brand, even in the offline world by just posting text and pictures. And these can be retweeted and liked by others.

Another singularity of social is that it's purely global — hashtags and posts are not limited to any country's borders — except a few ones like China, etc. which installed their networks. Only the language clusters the world into regions but in the end, all is public here and globally accessible. Returning to my client discussions, the main challenges I've seen there are two-fold. First the organizational topic: should there be a dedicated social team or is this capability part of the paid, owned, and earned teams that already exist? I prefer the choice to treat social as a capability and not as a team question. The second challenge is the effect within PEO-ROMI calculations. As there is always a shared effect in each bucket and the end, they can all be liked and shared, most of my clients struggled to attribute the social effects currently in their return on marketing investment calculations.

Voice needs to be seen in the same context; while social was the big hype of the early years of this century, 20 years later we have Deja Vue. The customer journey and touchpoints will be enhanced by several options. There are firstly the owned skills, podcasts, and bots; secondly, the paid pre/mid/end-rolls within voice streaming portals, the sponsoring of partner podcasts; and thirdly, the earned attention via influencers and voice search. Voice search itself is a special discipline that follows the strict paradigm: "the winner takes it all, second place first looser". This means your teams dealing with earned attention and/or search need to understand how the underlying algorithms of these voice devices work to be on top of all. Again for me, this looks more like a capability and not as an isolated channel within a paid, owned, and earned channel mix.

All of this is the reason why there's a dedicated ma.tomic on social and voice, succeeding in this domain means to build some kind of capability in several distinct areas.

Impact

- Social and voice capabilities enhance your activation mix on several touchpoints, thus your options for hyper-personalized customer experience increase, and by that also your conversions and customer loyalty.
- Being able to attribute voice and social effects to your activations allows you to better understand your actions and viral effects. Budget allocations can be optimized towards high converting channels and journeys.

Fields of Actions

- Treat social and voice as fundamental capabilities like e.g. digital and classic ad skills. Enhance your existing marketing target operating model with capabilities to service your clients also on social and voice.
- Design and implement shared and voice effects into your paid, owned, and earned return on marketing investment calculations.

IT Support and Platforms

- Social Listening Frameworks
- Social Engagement Clouds and Social CMS
- Voice Bot Frameworks
- Voice Commerce Frameworks

M8.5 Planning Pricing & Trade Promotions

There are further things we need to discuss within the domain of the innovative and optimized PEO activation mix. We have seen the classic paid, owned, and earned buckets; we discussed the two capabilities of social and voice, but we have not talked about the influence on marketing success due to sales are driving pricing, discount, and promotion strategies. Trade promotions or sales campaigns help to stimulate sales and to optimize margins. In most cases not seen as an essential part of marketing a full-blown strategic marketing planning also has to include the different sales activations.

Once, I met a CMO of a big electronic retailer who controlled the sales and performance campaigns of his worldwide stores. The discussion I had with him was eye-opening. He just joked that whenever he is running joined campaigns with the brands and suppliers his company is partnering with, he can influence the final success by smart use of trade promotions. In case, the campaign does not reach the expected goals, he just "pushed" them slightly by dealing with the prices and some trade promotions within the network of retail stores. Because of that, joined campaigns were always a success and the suppliers preferred his retail more in direct competition to others.

For that reason, I've added this special ma.tomic here; in detail, it includes the effects of data-driven pricing, trade promotions, and smart discounts on your marketing mix. As this is often controlled by different organizations outside of the standard marketing department, the main challenge is the sync of these customer interactions. Here the budgeting, preparation, and execution of each trade promotion, sales performance campaign, etc. needs to be aligned with the overall channel mix for paid, owned, and earned journeys to stay on top of mixed sales/marketing campaigns and activations.

Impact

- Alignment of sales and marketing campaigns (trade promotions, discounts, and data-driven pricing) avoid counteracting initiatives and can be used as a huge boost to your marketing activations.
- A holistic view on both sales and marketing activations avoid blurred KPIs by only focusing on one side of the medal.

Fields of Actions

- Establish a joined team and process to align marketing and sales activations in a close target operating model.
- Design and implement a closed-loop trade promotion process.

- Design and implement a closed-loop data-driven pricing process.
- Design and implement a joined reporting on marketing and sales success.

IT Support and Platforms

- Marketing planning platforms.
- Scenario planner for data-driven pricing simulations.
- Trade promotion planning systems.

M8.6 Media Mix Planning and Optimization

Once all the paid, owned, earned channels are planned and controlled and the sales activations are aligned, the next step is to optimize the spending on this mix. This means we don't treat them all in the same way; instead, we base on the audience we'd like to serve and the product we promote with the need to balance the investment into the different channels. The result is the best channel mix. This can be done by media mix planning and optimization on different levels. The overarching budgeting on paid, owned, earned, trade promotions, and within each of these buckets the distribution and optimization on the used channels.

For the high-level strategic allocation of budget, I've seen that the most successful clients I've met followed a really simple rule. When allocating the budget and resources, they used the 70-20-10 paradigm. Spend 70% on known channels and customer journeys, 20% on new but established ways of reaching the audience, and the last 10% on experiential ways of dealing with the customers and prospects; there has to be a static and agile mix. Most of the successful companies have established an agile target operating model within a strategic and most waterfall-based budgeting process. These setups allow us to define strategic investment directions by securing the necessary agility to reallocate money between the channels during the campaign and journey executions. This sandwich of top-down budget allocation and media-mix planning, plus the bottom-up real-time campaign and journey optimization including machine learning-based massive A/B testings, is the perfect setup for maximum conversions within your marketing funnel.

Impact

- Media mix modeling and optimization allows us to increase the overall and holistic effectiveness of the marketing spending.
- Media mix modeling allows to measure long-term effects on brand awareness (also from classical paid channels like TV, etc.) and by that saves high margins and customer loyalty
- Machine learning allows us to predict future optimizations automatically on a large scale.
- Real-time campaign and journey optimizations take care that the most effective activations are leveraged.

Fields of Actions

- Design and implement a top-down budget allocation and marketing mix modeling.
- Guarantee the freedom to have the flexibility to move budgets during campaign and journey execution.
- Install AI-based channel allocation algorithms.

IT Support and Platforms

- Marketing mix modeling and budget allocation platforms.
- Marketing planning platforms.

M9 GET VIRAL — SHARING ECONOMY OF SCALES

We have seen in the previous chapter of the ma.tomics the optimized PEO mix that includes these two capabilities: social and voice. I'd like to stress a bit more on the special effects of social media that have emerged at beginning of this century and helped to shape a new way of gaining and monitoring customer experience and interactions. With Facebook and the famous thumbs up button that represents one like, we have seen a phenomenon nobody has witnessed before. Suddenly there was something new! Somewhere between the total blindness and GRP-driven way of selling impressions on TV without knowing who has seen it and the strong behavioral trigger of clicking on a digital ad with a click-through URL using UTM parameters the like and share were invented.

Combined with the ways of following, posting, and sharing, a completely new layer allowed us to interact with customers in a much smoother way. While in the beginning, the social networks were used for information sharing within your private community of friends, the success attracted more and more brands to use the networks for their marketing activities also. This trend, together with the decision of Facebook to go for a closed business model, has been the initial advent of wallet gardens. Based on the model "give me your money, I'm going to do something great to you, the conversions will be 10 times higher," the triumphant march of the social networks began.

Within this section, I'd like to highlight two very important topics; the first is the fact, that everything can be liked, shared, and that there is a hidden data currency of #hashtags; the second ma.tomic here shows the necessity to deal with algorithms to analyze text, images by intelligent algorithms to track moods of social interactors.

M9.1 Tweets, Likes, and Shares

Let us start with the basics of social. Posting on a network means a "real" person or brand is uploading a combination of text, media (images, videos), and classifies it with hashtags. This now can be shared or liked by others — the result are viral network effects and millions on earned impressions. To earn money, the networks also allow the posting of "dark posts" that can't be seen on the brand canvas and they boost these kinds of posts with money to a pre-defined audience selection as a "suggested post."

Looking at this mini initial frame of reference we can pick out the parts that need to be managed within the ma.tomic. My educated guess is, that we do not have to talk much about text and content. There is only one thing I'd like to add; as everything can be posted and shared, we also have to take care of and analyze the social glut in the right way. This is the following ma.tomic of sentiment analysis and image recognition. But there is more than text and media — tweets are now including hashtags! Being involved with social means also dealing with hashtags in the right way. Find your unique and hopefully viral hashtags to classify your ecosystem is one of the things you need to master in this ma.tomic. Viral effects are the next thing we need to add here. As everything can be shared and liked, this ma.tomic also includes the right strategy of gaining maximum word of mouth and brand awareness in the social networks by combining smart boosting with broad fan and community management. Aside from this pure measurement of additional reach and success, the power of likes and shares needs to be part of the marketing planning. While shit storms can negatively influence the brand value, the opposite of viral communication about the products and work is also possible.

Social networks allow the customer to open communication with the company, thus a team and intelligent workflows have to be in place to handle the requests and posts with the minimal response time.

Impact

- Incorrectly answered social requests and posts can be the starting point of shit storms that destroy the brand value. Perfectly and rapidly handled customer requests will lead to perfect customer experience and journeys helping to increase word of mouth, brand value, and decreased churn rates.
- Scaling and fostering a community allows us to gain customer insights to serve dedicated audiences more efficiently.
- Likes and shares may generate viral network effects that end-up in millions of earned impressions.

Fields of Actions

- Design and install your social strategy, including hashtags, user access management, and viral strategies.
- Install scaling community management and smart customer request handling.

IT Support and Platforms

- Customer request platforms.
- Community clouds.
- Social engagement platforms.
- Creative assets clouds and master data management for hashtag management.

M9.2 AI Image Processing and Sentiment Analysis

I've mentioned it before, but you have the post or tweet and the surrounding hashtags, likes, and shares. Let's have a closer look at the content of the posts themselves. While the likes are a smart and easy way to show that you have perceived a message independently if you are happy or dissatisfied with it, there is the need to dig deeper into the real sentiment behind it. Clever AI algorithms analyze the text, images, and videos to extract the moods and atmosphere behind it. This can trigger internal workflows to react instantly on these posts. Furthermore, your reporting can be enhanced by further dimensions that split your reach into positive, neutral, and negative sentiments.

I've also seen successful implementations of AI image recognition for brands, that links the written text to the content of an image. For example, showing the logo of the brand can be detected by the algorithm and combined with the same classification I've shown above. This increases the requirements for your social listening platforms massively. It's no longer a simple hashtag filter engine. Instead, smart AI algorithms extract the essence of each post, trigger workflows within your customer service organization, and analyze these effects in your advanced data science

Impact

- Sentiment analysis analyzes the mood and atmosphere behind single posts and to react instantly. The effect is increased customer experience and loyalty.
- Sentiment analysis is a real-time mirror and feedback loop from the market linked to your marketing activities that optimize the efficiency of your activation strategies.

Fields of Actions

- Design and implement a sentiment scoring model and analysis framework.

IT Support and Platforms

- AI-driven social analytics platforms.

M10 THE MOST EFFECTIVE FLOW OF ACTIONS

The ma.tomics before have dealt a lot with planning budgets, finding the best channel mix, and generating viral effects. However, this has meant we have neglected the time dimension. The marketing-mix and channel optimizations used total aggregated numbers and conversions to find the best combinations. It's now the best opportunity for us to add time as a critical factor for perfect conversions.

As a physicist, time is magical, so bringing in this dimension will demonstrate that the schedule and flow of action are essential. Stepping away from the paradigm of "the last click wins" and focusing on single actions helps towards a more sophisticated attribution model, and will give you a better insight into how effective your channel mix works. If we start thinking about flows of actions, we also need to introduce the A/B testing topic again. The gravity wave of agility does not make any sense if we don't set up simultaneously running test scenarios to see which combination of actions runs the best. While standard A/B testing is still mostly manual installed testing, machine learning builds highly sophisticated decision trees, cluster analysis, and predictive next best actions on a massive scale.

Finally, I will close this chapter with two overarching topics: the first is fundamental (it's a pity that people in marketing do forget these good old masterpieces). Funnel and goal management never lost any glory as it gives all our attribution, journeys, and optimizations the frame to reduce complexity and to focus on the most effective next best actions. Secondly, I'd like to raise an idea based on Isaac Newton's law of actions. If we could measure the correct attribution and effects of our activations, why not flip the scene upside down and start planning on outcomes to calculate the necessary budget to reach these goals? This means time and then reverse the time by start planning for the outcome is for me the most exciting piece of marketing besides the revolution of real customer-centric and data-driven thinking. Let us jump into this topic to see how real math-men master the time challenge.

M10.1 Multi-Touch Attribution Models

The first time we see the effect of time is by not taking care of the exact moment of interactions; instead, we're just sequencing all actions on a timeline. This gives us a flow of actions that achieve a dedicated conversion or success. We attribute this success measure no longer to one single interaction, instead, it is to the total flow of actions. The last click wins mentality was the most prominent paradigm seen in marketing. Millions of dollars were spent on search as people did not tend to click on banners or other ads. Instead, they are influenced to remember the call-to-action. Naturally, they start searching for the product or service via a search engine. And bang, the easy deductive reasoning is to think search is more powerful than any other activation.

Modern marketing technology stack tracks impressions and customer behavior on single interactions. Thus they also allow us to build a flow of actions on how people run through your funnel. And here we see that for sure in the upper funnel also display, social and video have a huge share in attracting prospects. We also see that our investment in owned touchpoints, personalizations, etc. is worth it, as it also helps to burn the message into the customer's mind. This means these kinds of following your audience across their journey through your defined marketing funnel based on big data marketing clouds is also the advent of attribution models.

Today we see that there are more than ten different ways of attributing the success of your marketing interactions instead of the most famous last click wins we have seen at the beginning of this century. Your business model, way of marketing and desired outcomes decide which is the best one for you:

- The first touch or lead generation attribution.
- The last touch attribution.
- Linear distribution.
- Time decay attribution.
- Position Based/U-, W- or Z-Shaped Attribution.
- Algorithmic attribution.

Impact

- Analysis of the flow of actions in attribution models allocates the marketing budget to the most efficient combination of actions and increases the total conversion rates.
- Analysis of the flow of actions allows us to understand the customer better and for that reason, to ultimately optimize how to interact with them to increase the customer experience, loyalty, and conversions.

Fields of Actions

- Design and implement an enterprise-wide and cross-system taxonomy.
- Overarching cross-system design and implementation of a comprehensive audience-centric data lake including all relevant actual and success data on a single event-log level.
- Design and implement (predictive) attribution models according to your business and marketing model.

IT Support and Platforms

- Data management platforms.
- Customer database platforms and real-time event tracking systems.
- Analytics platforms and predictive model frameworks.
- Master data management and governance platforms.
- Reporting, explorative, and data science platforms.

M10.2 Large Scale A/B testing & 1:1 journeys

As we now have introduced the time dimension to define the flow of actions to attribute success in the previous ma.tomic, we can further enhance this concept. Instead of using a single sequence of actions, we can now start to change parts of the sequence or, even better, run multiple in parallel to see which one works the best.

Large scale A/B testing is exactly doing this. While we have seen previously in the ma.tomic about agile target operating models, we can use A/B testing to try out what works best is a single touchpoint, e.g. which picture or navigation attracts the desired audience the best, so now we expand this idea further. Instead of optimizing only one touchpoint, we use the tests on a large-scale to test which flow of actions works the best. Going further down this road of personalization and testing, we end up with a 100% personalized customer journey. The tests, algorithms, and attribution will work perfectly so that everybody in our audience is treated in a one-on-one way. Artificial intelligence and machine learning can help to massively scale up the number of tests without eating up the labor forces.

This means also going fully away from the old mad-men style of doing marketing and using data as the only basement for all your decisions.

Impact

- The use of large scale A/B testing allows us to identify the most efficient flow of actions and increase the conversions of each campaign and customer journey.
- The use of data-driven insights allows us to replace the gut feeling for perfect customer experience with far more efficient data-driven decisions.

Fields of Actions

- Design and implementation of a marketing automation framework to activate campaigns and journeys via all customer touchpoints in a highly personalized way.
- Design and implement large scale and cross-platform A/B testing infrastructure based on the used marketing technology stack.

IT Support and Platforms

- Data management platforms and customer database platform.
- Real-time event tracking systems.
- Dynamic creative optimization, A/B testing, and personalization frameworks.
- Analytics platforms and predictive model frameworks.

M10.3 Machine Learning — AI-Driven Optimizations

The end of John Wanamaker's famous statement does ring true with data: "Half the money he spends on advertising is wasted; the trouble is he does not know which half."

Machine learning enables you to save money by using it and it's the ultimate hype in the modern marketing setup of the 2020s. But I've also seen into the inner operating model of most huge advertisers of the world. Trust me, there isn't a single one that is using AI out of the box to harvest this added value by the marketing platform vendors. This is hard work and the last step in a long chain of fundamental steps that need to be in place before really benefiting from AI in marketing.

I've often used comparisons when talking with my clients about the power of machine learning. If it was easy, everybody would just sign the license contract of one of the prominent AI platforms, and all is done — bang — tripled marketing output with the same budget! Unfortunately, this is not the case; using AI in marketing is a competitive advantage you need to earn with hard work. You need to build a high-performing marketing machine first and balanced the set up out of target operating model of data-driven processes, highly skilled teams, and big data IT platforms; you need to choose where AI can help to further tune-up this engine.

The most exciting fields of actions to use machine learning in marketing are:

- Audience segmentation is based on clusters and relationship algorithms.
- Demand forecastings based on regression algorithms.
- Conversion optimizations and real-time interaction design based on decision trees (e.g. time spend, splits, programmatic ad targeting, dynamic content optimization, SEO, pattern recognition).
- Lead scorings.
- Churn scoring and predictions.
- Trade promotion management based on Monte Carlo simulations.
- Data-driven pricing.
- Next best action predictions and propensity scorings.
- Competitive benchmarking based on social listening.

Impact

- The use of artificial intelligence in the form of different algorithms allows us to avoid using a human's gut feeling towards a purely data-driven approach of permanently generated insights and optimized marketing activations — this allows marketing efficiencies up to three times higher compared to human decision-based activations.

Fields of Actions

- Design and implement a machine learning infrastructure and integrate it into your comprehensive paid, owned, and earned marketing technology stack
- Transform your human decision-based way of executing marketing towards a data-driven way based on algorithms where ever possible.

- Abandon yourself and your organization from the illusion that AI automatically will optimize your marketing, the key success is to identify the fields of actions where your target operating model benefits from machine learning.

IT Support and Platforms

- Predictive and AI-based frameworks.
- Integration frameworks into the marketing technology stack.

M10.4 Goal and Funnel management

In an agile world, we all know that the success of a single strategic marketing program is not reached within a single execution of a campaign. Even if we optimized our flow of actions perfectly through massive testing and AI — prospects and customers are still humans at the end of the day! They will take tiny steps back and forth, being indecisive, so we need to guide them over various subsequent campaign goals towards our final desired overarching program success.

This means our program not only defines the final goal and correlated KPIs, but will also design the funnel of actions to be successful. For example, we could try to enhance the awareness of our product, then motivate prospects to do some research on the details and specifications to finally attract our future customers to buy the product in our online store. This might be seen as old-fashioned funnel logic, but I'm deeply convinced that in our complex world of paid, owned, and earned touchpoints, the funnel is the only way to stay on top of your journeys and to define an overarching grid for the program, campaign, and journey goals.

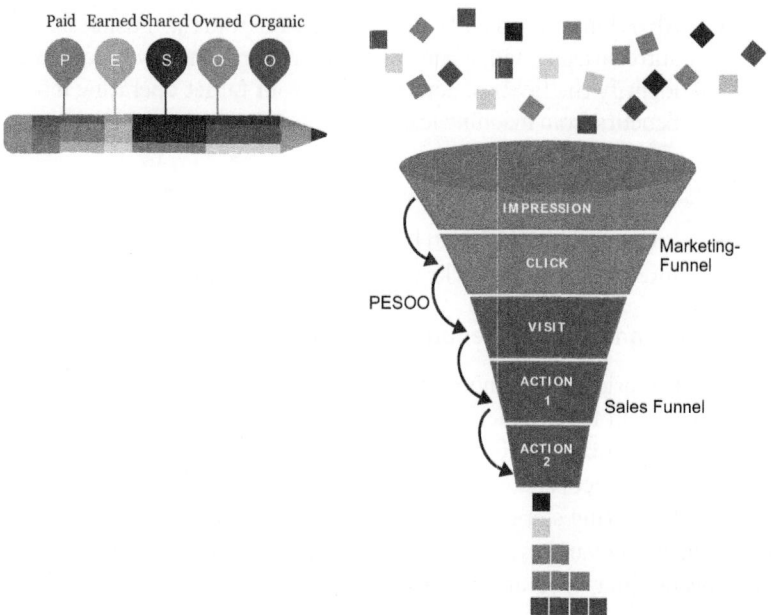

The winning formula for success is to combine the goal and funnel concept as a top-down driven approach based on a waterfall model with a bottom-up customer journeys management. In such a model, push campaigns are used to move the audience from one point to another or to avoid bouncing out of the existing flow of actions. The marketing leaders I was allowed to consult were all precisely aware of the best fitting funnel and how to drive audiences through the different layers. Finally, this all is the basement for real-time analysis of customer events and AI-based feedback in form of personalizations and recommendations as described in the previous ma.tomic.

Impact

- Tailoring overarching goals into smaller actions will increase the single conversion rates as the hurdles to step in for customers get eliminated — overall conversions will increase.
- Automatic journeys reduce the manual effort to push out campaigns within a defined sequence, thus operating costs are reduced.
- A better customer experience due to perfectly orchestrated triggers and actions will end up with higher customer satisfaction, less churn, and an enhanced customer lifetime value.

Fields of Actions

- Implement a goal and funnel concept within the strategic marketing planning.
- Use the funnel as an overarching grid within your PESO ROMI dashboards and analytics.
- Design and implement customer journeys within the marketing automation to drive your audience through the flow of actions.
- Set up a monitoring and governance process on the usage of funnels and goals.

IT Support and Platforms

- Marketing planning platforms that make use of different planning layers and allow to define program goals and related funnels.
- PESO dashboards.

M10.5 The Law of Action and Reaction — High Performing Machines

At the very end of developing a perfect marketing flow of actions, use of machine learning to optimize the touchpoints, sequences of the touchpoints, and the orchestration across the funnel, we can think about reverting the time dimension.

If we trust in Newton's law about action and reaction, we can design a marketing universe where we start with the desired outcomes and thinking upside down. Every action is a part of a reaction paradigm. Thus, we can use the reaction as the desired outcome and think about what related action is necessary to enforce this reaction. This action is, again, a reaction of a second step before and so on. This means the budgeting, goals, funnels, and journeys are the starting point of our planning instead of the outcome and we think about the cause and effect of every action within our funnel.

This is the opposite of how we have thought and worked so far. Instead of starting to model the final results, we'd like to reach (e.g. 1000 products sold with total revenue of x and margin of y dollars) and using systems to leverage machine learning algorithms to find out the right mix of campaigns, the perfect sub-goals within the funnel and finally, the flow of actions we should push our audience in we start working on the final goals we'd like to reach. Such high performing machine learning-based marketing machines are highly automated. For most of us, known marketing organizations move away from a craft worker towards a manager pursuing enterprise business goals and controlling the machine's behavior and outputs. Marketing is no longer a cost center; it is the innovation center pulling audiences into our enterprise eco-system and converts them into customers and fans.

Impact

- By turning the classic approach of budgeting upside down the organization gets truly data-driven with a pure focus on the outcome and customer experience.
- All of the conversion optimizations are highly efficient and fully supported by machine learning and predictive algorithms.

Fields of Actions

- Design and implement an enterprise-wide taxonomy and cause-effect flow within your marketing funnel.
- Implement machine learning not only within single touchpoints, instead use algorithms to optimize the full flow of actions through the entire funnel and journey.

IT Support and Platforms

- N/A: this is all about orchestrating existing technology in a best-working way.

M11 CUSTOMER INTIMACY — DEMAND WINDOWS AND PRICING

We have seen in the previous chapter that the huge power the introduction of a time dimension has on the way we optimize our marketing universe; funnels, journeys, attribution, and marketing mix modeling only works if we move away from single conversion optimization towards a sequence or flow of actions. However, different systems of reference have different time systems; all is relative. There is only one constant; the speed of light. Before we have a more in-depth look at light speed in marketing, let's see if we have tackled all the topics around time.

All the optimizations above have one assumption in common: the individual in our audience is a fully predictable human being, and cause and effect can be modeled based on historic behavioral data, and comparisons to digital twins and what they have done. We all know this is not true; the behavior of our audience we like to reach is highly dependent on the context we reach them. This means, where, when, and which price proposals are given is essential for every buying decision or related action in the upper funnel. With this ma.tomic I will have a look at the initial frame of reference from our most "unknown" piece in the marketing universe — the prospect and customer themselves and the demand windows where some things may work and others not.

M11.1 Find the Right Moment in Time — Demand Windows

Demand windows focus on the time dimension within the customer experience. Most attribution models analyze the flow and sequence of actions but don't consider the correct moment to place the right flow of actions.

Just think about an attribution example in the upper funnel; our algorithms optimized to a flow of actions digital display › social › voice › search › personalized splash screens works the best. Looking back, we can assume the following hypothesis: the prospect gets attracted by digital banners on his favorite newspaper page. Later, as he takes the subway to work, he can be reached via social networks and voice pre-rolls. Once he's at work, he only just remembers the great product and uses a search engine to finally end up on our homepage with the splash screen showing a discount voucher that he should use immediately. However, this only works if we start the journey in the morning. If we were to start in the evening with the digital displays, we will lose him as overnight he is not online, so the next morning, he has forgotten all about it. Therefore, timing is crucial to deliver the message and call to action. This will allow us to optimize the best fitting demand windows, and applying massive A/B testing and artificial intelligence is the secret tool to add to it.

Impact

- Taking the initial frame of reference of your customer into consideration leverages the best buying moments to increase the conversions and customer experience.

Fields of Actions

- Design and implement customer analytics including the time dimension.
- Implement machine learning not only in single touchpoints, instead, use algorithms to optimize the demand window of your entire funnel and journey.

IT Support and Platforms

- N/A: this is all about orchestrating existing technology in the best way.

M11.2 Find the best context — Demand Windows

There is more than time to consider once taking the initial frame of reference of our prospects and customers into consideration. For our buying decisions and likelihood to accept any recommendations also the context in form of the location, surrounding people and environment, etc. is important. It needs to be analyzed and used when implementing demand windows as well as the time dimension. For that reason, there is also a context-based demand window that needs to be analyzed by tracking the ecosystem around the customer whenever he interacts with the company or brand.

Let me point out here two main aspects of the context-based demand windows, first the location and second, the effect of surrounding people. Location is similar to the time dimension a trend of the last years and can be tracked via mobile smartphone App data, near-field Bluetooth beacons, WIFI access-points, or less precise by text or image recognitions (e.g. mountain shapes, landmarks, etc.).

It opens a broad bunch of different use-cases for the modern marketeer. For example, splash screens in owned apps can provide discount vouchers once somebody enters the inner circle around your retail store. Or in multilayer sales setups where product produces do not have their point of sales, they can guide people to the next physical store from their distribution network in their call to action.

I've seen a lot of really great and super effective use-cases, this is one of the reasons why I see the location-based demand windows as a strong differentiator to take you apart from your competitors. Secondly, the context-based demand window is somehow leveraging the swarm intelligence of social crowds. We are heavily influenced by the people around us and their actions. If someone likes a movie, buys a product, etc. these are often strong triggers for us to act similarly. This is the reason why nearly all online shops use recommendations of "people who bought this have also bought this," or the use of recommendations and ratings at the checkout.

So, let us keep in mind for this ma.tomic, that aside from the time-driven demand window there is a second playground we need to understand in detail and which opens a broad variety of powerful marketing use-cases.

Impact

- Taking the initial frame of reference of your customer into consideration leverages the best buying moments to increase the conversions and customer experience.

Fields of Actions

- Design and implement customer analytics including the location, social interaction, and other behavioral and contextual dimensions.
- Implement machine learning not only with single touchpoints, instead use algorithms to optimize the demand window of your entire funnel and journey.

IT Support and Platforms

- Location-based tracking platforms.
- Social interaction tracking platforms.

M11.3 Find the Best Price — Data-Driven Pricing Windows

Aside from the correct timing and context, the price is one of the most powerful tools to optimize the marketing return on investment and influence buying decisions. As an essential part of the marketing mix and one of the four Ps (place, product, promotion, price) it is clear that pricing is a ma.tomic of its own that needs to be considered in your marketing activations and target operating models.

Each marketing transformation initiative has to include a data-driven pricing stream to implement across the sales channels. Data-driven pricing is based on two pillars: the first is the design of the appropriate model and attributes to calculate prices; the second is the consequent massive A/B testing and the use of predictive models to optimize the pricing engine based on the upfront defined attributes. A well-known example would be searching for flights, music events, holiday locations, etc. on the internet. Based on the used hardware (e.g. Apple Macbooks) the initial price is set and then slightly increased with each repeated search. The third, maximum fourth, time people search a specific topic they have the highest propensity also to buy the ticket.

This sounds logical and easy to implement, however, from what I've seen during the last few years, this ma.tomic has been placed firmly in second place. My educated guess is that the implementation needs a very strong, interconnected process alignment between the marketing and sales organization. This is not the case very often, however; in most companies, the two departments still act as two separate teams. The second reason might be that the business experience and technical infrastructure for data-driven pricing can be very complex. The integration into finance and controlling is a key challenge that needs to be overcome. Thus, CMOs need to invest long-term in an operating model without gaining fast returns.

Impact

- Finding the best fitting pricing model will increase the conversions and bottom-line margin.
- AI algorithms optimize the weights against the maximum yield by balancing price and conversions.

Fields of Actions

- Design and implement a dynamic and data-driven pricing model, including the aligned target operating model between sales and marketing.
- Design and implement the model within your marketing technology stack and commerce infrastructure.

IT Support and Platforms

- CPQ and data-driven pricing frameworks (configure, price, quote).
- Dynamic pricing integration into the finance and controlling domain.

M12 CROSS DEVICE AND PLATFORMS

Looking at what analysts and platform vendors claim, all ma.tomics can be implemented with a few clicks and subscriptions via comprehensive marketing clouds; it can be just that simple. However, in the last 20 years, I have not seen a single advertiser mastering all the requirements with one single platform in a green-field implementation. Instead, most target operating models are set up on an imperfect patchwork of different historically used marketing platforms. Setups like this imply that the holy grail of end-to-end journeys and the funnel we guide our customers through will not work. The simple reason behind this is that we can't identify across our used platforms that profile A in platform X is the same person as profile B in system Y. To be very honest, this is the easy part of this ma.tomic. In the end, it is the consequent implementation of your ID, consent and profile strategy, and technology platform. On the other hand, there is the customer with his various devices. Cross identification within your marketing universe is divided in the upper cross-platform challenger but also includes the cross-device topic.

People tend to use a minimum of two to three devices, but in some cases, there could be more than that used. Therefore your setup must also allow the merging of several devices and their IDs into one profile instead of treating them as distinct pieces in your flow of actions. So-called customer 360° systems that take the advantage of graph databases need to be put below your activation stack. This will guarantee whatever identifier your customers use (cookie, IFA, email, phone, log in, etc.) all the interactions will be combined in one single profile.

M12.1 Cross-Device Identification — ID Strategies

The ma.tomic of cross-device identification is about aggregating different devices used by one person in a single profile, but this also works vice versa, as one device can be used by two or more people attributed to the correct profile in question. Both challenges can be mastered by a consequent ID strategy definition and implementation. Instead of tracking user behavior on the unique IDs of devices the user needs to provide a unique key independent from the touchpoint he is using.

This is the best strategy, though especially in the upper funnel or for specific business models like consumer goods are not always possible. The only way of tracking users and building profiles is the use of cookies and mobile identifiers. For these cases, graph databases serve as the base for DMPs (data management platform) and CDPs (customer data platforms) and help to build-up profiles step by step. Each interaction on a touchpoint is first tracked towards a specific ID; this can be in the upper funnel cookies, IFAs, and further down the road, logins, emails, phone numbers, etc. In case the ID is a known one, the system attributes the action towards the profile, in case the ID is new, a new profile is also generated. The graph itself is used to combine profiles in a new merged version. To optimize this merging mechanism, the ID strategy tries to gather more than one ID within an action in the customer journey. Just think about a login screen on a wifi welcome screen that asks for your email, this allows to combine cookie, email and in case that several devices are used also to build a cross-device graph. This kind of deterministic device ID tracking is the most accurate and should be used and implemented wherever possible. There is a second AI-based option to merge profiles in a graph database based on algorithms. This way of probabilistic device ID tracking uses a full bunch of different attributes to cluster devices based on their:

- Fingerprints (operating systems, screen resolutions, installed fonts, browser versions, installed apps, etc.).
- WIFI zones.
- Geo locations.
- Behavioral and browsing data.
- Time zones.
- IP addresses.

Every use of probabilistic IDs needs its own methodology and algorithm. Well-reputed companies that develop probabilistic IDs may boast 70%-95% accuracy (compared to deterministic IDs) in the upper funnel where "real deterministic" IDs are mostly rare. Let's return to the example above where we asked for a login for the confirmation to use a public WIFI network to combine cookie and email address. We can also use this WIFI point in combination with timestamps to see that two devices always login/log out at the same time, without logging into the network. This means even without using the network, the meta pieces of information allow us to build a graph between the mobile and laptop as they always appear at the same time in our WIFI zone.

ID mapping also helps to keep profiles healthy and actual. Even if a cookie dies, the use of several identifiers and the ongoing merging into one profile does save your data from being outdated and builds a competitive advantage in the form of a profile database that can be used for segmentation and activations within push campaigns and customer journeys.

This ma.tomic is one of the most exciting and also volatile I've seen over the last 10 years. The speed of innovation in technology and AI is high and the counteraction of legal constraints follow slightly shifted back. Thus data-driven organizations and CMOs need to master this field in an ongoing change to stay on top of innovations and also to always stay in line with legal and legitimate constraints. Together with the ma.tomic "M6 — Profiling" is the fundamental base for perfect segmentation and customer journey management.

Impact

- Cross-device identification allows to merge profile, this deepens the insights about single customers and prospects to optimize user experience, conversion, and bounce rates.
- The cross-device graph also allows to build long-term profiles by the frequent update, this helps to build a competitive advantage of a huge customer database platform.
- Cross-device profiles allow an overarching frequency capping and by that reduces wasted impressions.

Fields of Actions

- Design and implement an enterprise/eco-system wide ID strategy.
- Design and implement deterministic profile mapping within your DMP and CDP.
- Design and implement various probabilistic algorithms to merge profiles in the upper funnel.

IT Support and Platforms

- Graph databases within DMPs and CDPs.
- Probabilistic merging algorithms.

M12.2 Cross-Platform Profiles

Let us briefly recall the ma.tomics of the chapter "M6 Profiling". The idea is to set up two fundamental profiles in the upper and lower funnel in a data management and customer data platform (DMP/CDP) to provide a comprehensive customer 360 profile as the foundation for the segmentation in campaigns and customer journeys.

But the marketing universe and technology stack is one of the most complex and fragmented in the enterprise software domain. While in the ERP backend, there is a standard for most interfaces, the advertising, and owned experience stack is not that clear. First, legal constraints enforce vendors to change their data storage and interfaces frequently. The power of "wallet gardens" in the advertising industry is far more powerful. Since Facebook has decided not to open its ecosystem, and instead of running a closed advertising system driven by above-average conversions but does not allow to track audiences, the idea of customer 360 profiles was challenged massively.

In a perfect world, we would follow the path of the profiling ma.tomics and cross-device enhancements, but the reality enforces us to use multiple systems to personalize the perfect customer journey. Just remember that the long list of possible paid, owned, and earned touchpoints have been described above. This enforces us to install a similar pattern as we have seen in the cross-device ma.tomic. There is a type of leading customer 360 CDP/DMP that is connected to all marketing systems, which is used to contact prospects and customers. This means we enhance our ID strategy further and besides the cross-device idea, we also merge profiles across our owned and paid technology stack. There is also a need to install cross-platform ID strategies since legal constraints like end-to-end consent management and the right of the customer to ask for data or deletion of them can only be efficiently handled with this kind of setup. A central customer 360 platforms as a master system and satellites of activation systems on top that are synchronized to the central entity.

Impact

- Cross-platform identification allows us to merge profiles; this deepens the insights about single customers and prospects to optimize user experience, conversion, and bounce rates.
- A custom 360 platform providing cross-platform profiles allows us to build long-term profiles by the frequent update. This helps to build a competitive advantage of a huge customer database platform.
- Cross-platform profiles allow an overarching frequency capping and by that reduces wasted impressions.

Fields of Actions

- Design and implement an enterprise/eco-system wide ID strategy and master/satellite profile technology stack (customer 360 architecture).

IT Support and Platforms

- Customer 360 profile architecture and integration.

M13 MEASURE REACH, SUCCESS & AWARENESS

Now, we are two-thirds of the way through all of the ma.tomics. We have covered the fundamental marketing universe with mandatory budgeting processes, the paradigm of running fast to failing fast in an agile environment, and the core ma.tomics of profiling and marketing mix to activate perfect customer journeys.

It's time to turn our attention towards the measurement of reach and related success. If we trust on the statement that only data matters, we need to know how many people we have reached and what kind of success we generated in each funnel layer and touchpoint. The comparison between the necessary costs and the final output is nothing short of the holy grail we are all looking for — the marketing return on investment KPI (ROMI).

The ma.tomics are all about calculating the reach within your marketing universe and in the case of success, what happened in the three buckets of awareness: eCom plus direct digital customer interactions (D2C — direct to customer/consumer) and in your offline "brick and mortar retail" point of sales ecosystem. While a general measurement and attribution of your actual impressions towards the success on your owned platform is today state-of-the-art and provided by nearly all digital analytics platforms, I've seen challenges in the implementation of more granular setups. Translating your top-down marketing planning into an agile campaign and journey execution enforces us to use IDs and taxonomies to attribute on lowest level success data to actual impression and planned values. The nitty-gritty implementation of central campaign IDs and strict master data governance secures your success.

In 1973, Peter Drucker wrote, "... because the purpose of any business is to create a customer, the business has two — and only two — basic functions: innovation and marketing. Marketing and Innovation produce results, all the rest are costs."

While his quote demonstrates a bit of "black and white thinking," there is one fundamental truth in it; independent from the perfect flow of actions and excellent conversions in the lower funnel, if we don't fill the first layer with reach, we can't generate new prospects and customers! This is the reason why I'd like to start with the ma.tomic of integrated reach, which is a calculated KPI out of the measure Reach1+ in every activation channel. Tracking this integrated reach as the ongoing flow of people into your marketing funnel is your first step into a data-driven marketing universe and a huge step from a mad-men towards a math-men. To put it in layman's terms, it's a bit like a central speed meter in the middle of your car console.

M13.1 Integrated Reach

If we trust in the paradigm that there is first awareness before anything else, which is generated by reaching out to any strategic audiences with marketing messages and relying on our initial frame of reference. With this, there is a very strong need to measure reach and frequency. As aforementioned previously, we have seen the idea of using the laws of fluid dynamics and treat our initial frame of reference like a closed-loop pipe system, which is where liquid in the form of campaigns and journeys run through various speeds; these speeds depend on the diameter of our pipe pieces. In such a Gedankenexperiment, "integrated reach" is the main valve at the very beginning of the closed-loop pipe system. It defines how many people we can pull into our marketing universe and the initial pressure we put on our target operating model. Just think about the reverse: without reach in the upper funnel, nobody would be aware of your brand and products, thus nobody will be interested in them or want them. In an audience-driven universe, it isn't that complex as piggybacked beacons allow us to track single events that we can then attribute to our profiles. This can be used in big data calculations to count the unique prospects and customers we have seen in each touchpoint. As well as this, we can accumulate these numbers across our dimension tree of markets, campaigns, creatives, etc. to finally get an estimation of our total integrated reach within each funnel layer.

Unfortunately, the marketing universe is not that easy, after all — there are several galaxies, at the very least. In our first Gedankenexperiment, we witnessed the difference between context and audience-centric universes. For those unaware, customer-centric and data-driven math-men marketing means using single customer interactions and ID strategies to calculate a precise reach across all devices of our customers and platforms that we use as a brand. Other galaxies in our marketing universe do not allow this kind of tracking, unfortunately; classic channels like TV, Radio, Cinema, etc. provide only aggregated numbers in form of GRPs. Or wallet gardens like social networks often provide us only aggregated reach numbers.

With the Sainsbury formula, which was invented in Britain to estimate reach across channels, we can monitor the total audience reached across each funnel layer. The method assumes that exposure is a Bernoulli process, meaning it follows a binomial distribution. The method can be stated as follows: $Rm = 1 - (1 - p1)(1 - p2)(1 - p3) \ldots (1 - pm)$ where: Rm = reach of "m" vehicles in a schedule with one insertion in each vehicle. pi = the audience of the vehicle "i" expressed as a percentage of the target market size.

Impact

- Integrated reach determines a realistic reach of unique prospects and customers within the paid, owned and earned marketing universe to optimize the spend and marketing pressure we'd like to pursue.
- Controlling integrated reach is like controlling the main valve in your closed-loop campaign and journey management and running your target operating model at the maximum speed.

Fields of Actions

- Design and implement a comprehensive audience-centric data lake including all relevant actual and successful data in combination with campaign-related aggregated reach data.
- Design and implement approximation models (Bernoulli theorem) to predict the integrated reach for all context centric touchpoints that do not allow to track single-user interactions.

IT Support and Platforms

- Data management platforms and customer database platform.
- Real-time event tracking systems (piggybacked impression beacons).
- ETL and analytics platforms including predictive model frameworks.

M13.2 Brand Awareness

If we follow Newton's law of 'action equals reaction,' we need to see some effects on every impression we have sent out into our marketing universe. While performance campaigns and journeys make it easy to assign success directly to the invested budget (ROMI), for brand campaigns, this is much more complex. To measure success in this domain, which is in the upper funnel, we need to track brand awareness. This is often done via time-consuming, expensive surveys based on panels and target groups. Attributing it to a dedicated campaign or journey is a further challenge and depends on the frequency of the surveys and time correlations that attribute incremental uplifts. A new trend in the industry is to alter this time and budget intensive way by replacing the feedback out of the panels with social listening data. Having access to millions of public data sources allows us to track prospects and customers by measuring brand awareness, image strength, and brand relevance in near real-time. This allows sophisticated models and algorithms to calculate the brand value on a monetary basis, to use it similar to performance metrics in a ROMI calculation. Other prominent KPIs reflect the willingness of the reached audience to recommend the product or brand, the most known and used is the "net promoter score."

Impact

- Brand valuation allows us to calculate ROMI for brand campaigns to use similar optimization strategies we normally use within performance campaigns and journeys.
- High awareness values allow us to optimize margins through data-driven price strategies.

Fields of Actions

- Design and implement brand awareness measurement processes and tools (survey-based).
- Design and implement a public data screening and listening platform and strategy.
- Design and implement a brand valuation model and algorithm.

IT Support and Platforms

- Market survey platform and panel-based screening platforms.
- Digital intelligence platforms for public data screening.
- Analytics platforms including predictive model frameworks.

M13.3 eCom — Direct to customer models

Welcome to the ma.tomic where data-driven marketing is born. Converting awareness into direct sales via e-Commerce models has been established since the .com bubble beginning of this century. We have all seen Amazon rising through the ranks to become one of the biggest online retail giants by disrupting several historic retail business models. For the ma.tomics model, I've broadened the e-Commerce model to a direct-to-customer (D2C) set up that also includes all digital touchpoints providing services besides the classic shop platforms to sell products via the internet.

The charm of D2C in marketing is how easy it is to attribute success data to all other actual and plan data. Technically, based on piggybacked beacons, click-trackers, and UTM parameters, each conversion within our customer journey can be tracked in DMPs, CMP, and digital analytics platforms. These conversions include the downloading of papers, subscriptions to newsletters, webinars, movie views, and downloads, etc. besides the selling of products in the lower end of our marketing and sales funnel.

In the early ma.tomics of M3 for the marketing program management and M5, including agile campaign management, it has been demonstrated that bigger brands typically deal with a bunch of simultaneously executed journeys and campaigns. While the attribution of success towards the initial impression or journey step is an easy technical task, it is the allocation towards the overarching structures of campaigns and programs that presents the real challenge. The best target operating models I've seen that have mastered this is the consequent use of piggybacked IDs in a strict taxonomy. For example, let's assume we have defined some marketing programs, A, B, and C — each with multiple campaigns and journeys 1, 2, 3, and further down the road, there are different touchpoints and marketing assets (x, y, and z) used via multiple providers (YT, DD, IG). It needs to be guaranteed through master data management and governance that all the interactions include a unique code that looks like this: A, 1, X, YT. This code is piggybacked on each impression as a beacon tracked via a DMP or CDP and also part of all API calls, click-trackers, and UTM/URL parameters to attribute the success to the correct activation.

As always, the problem with this is not the type of technology used; we have seen UTM and all the other tracking options for decades. The main challenges are the humans and the target operating model. Brands that can align dozen of parties like owned teams, agencies, influencers, etc. in their complex paid, owned, and earned marketing universe to consistently tag all actions with the latest IDs will be the leaders; ultimately, the laggers are going to sink in mountains of chaotically stored data points, with seemingly no way out.

Impact

- Direct-to-customer business models allow you to enhance your current way to interact with prospects and customers to increase the digital experience and allow e-commerce options for product/service check-outs.
- D2C models will leverage the intelligent data-driven core capabilities of hyper-accurate targeted personalization and recommendations, this will end up in significant higher conversions, scaled digital sales, and ROMI.

Fields of Actions

- Ideate, design and implement a direct to customer business setup for our existing business model.
- Design and implement a commerce platform and integrate a strict tagging and success measurement.
- Design a central campaign ID taxonomy and include the use in all of the activations and customer interactions.

IT Support and Platforms

- Commerce cloud.
- Experience cloud.

M13.4 Offline — Retail — Brick and Mortar Models

Similar to the challenge of how to measure awareness it's the "old economy" of brick and mortar business that is offline in most cases. With the advent of the internet of things and always connected sensors, the new "digitized" store concepts allow integration in the offline world. Based on connected products, Bluetooth beacons, WIFI hotspots, image recognition, etc. different success and actual metrics can be assigned to marketing programs and campaigns.

However, it is the customer identification, legal consent management for tracking, and the rollout to an existing retail universe that are often huge challenges that need to be faced. The most successful setups I've seen were modern cashier systems, combined with loyalty programs and customer cards. The systems need to be integrated into the final check-out process at a point of sale; they also need to be connected in real-time to the data-driven marketing back-end. Looking at our initial frame of reference, we should act in the offline galaxy similarly to how we would act in the digital galaxy. Therefore, the first phase is mostly focused on collecting success data, though the real benefits will be generated by implementing personalization and recommendation models within the connected store concepts. To give an example, the displays in retail spaces are used to recommend products and push personalized messages as they're the first thing the customers see when they step into the store.

This ma.tomic includes another factor that we should consider as we transform our thinking from mad-men marketing to math-men marketing. Even if your point-of-sales isn't digitalized, you can still digitalize your products. For example, in a retail business that is completely offline, customers may purchase a product that needs to be activated via an online channel, that offers participation within an online sweepstake, or other things — whenever there's a way to use a digital touchpoint after a customer has purchased an item, you should make use of it so you can provide the additional support you can; you attribute this product to a digital profile ID and by that, you close the loop of customer-centric and data-driven marketing.

Impact

- Integrating the offline "brick and mortar" retail business into the data-driven backend allows us to assign both successful and actual data to the campaigns to calculate a realistic ROMI. This helps to optimize budget decisions and the marketing mix.
- Personalizations and recommendations frameworks within connected retail spaces lead to higher conversions and sales revenues in the "offline" galaxy.
- Perfect orchestrated offline/online customer journey will lead to higher customer satisfaction and less churn/bounce on the edge from online to offline.
- Digitized "products" help to attribute to the success of offline sales towards online campaigns and journeys.

Fields of Actions

- Design and implement actual and successful data gathering within the offline world.
- Design and implement a connected and digitized retail space and experience.
- Digitize products in an offline galaxy of retail spaces.

IT Support and Platforms

- Internet of things platforms.
- Perfect storage of infrastructure and beacons.
- Use of QR codes and other "quick" access options to an online digital marketing galaxy.

M13.5 General — Market Intelligence and Surveys

For a long time, there has been much debate, and even I struggled with it, is the concept of if a general ma.tomic for market intelligence is still necessary for the modern-day. Intelligent data-driven marketing is all about planning top-down programs and executing them in a streamlined, agile, and bottom-up approach; this would solely optimize the data points gathered during the execution and in your owned ecosystem. There would be a complete focus on awareness and performance metrics in a comprehensive end-to-end return on marketing investment (ROMI) setup.

Therefore, why do we need to ask customers through a panel, which is what they used to do in the early days of mad-men marketing? However, Panes and Survefy are extremely expensive pieces of software; they're also slow in responsiveness, which shows our planned success metrics. To be honest, to talk about measuring success without talking about market intelligence would not be right because even the best behavioral tracking and social listening sometimes need to be confirmed or enhanced by asking your real prospects and customers! Over the years, this used to be the only way to generate success data, and still, panel-based surveys and focus group interviews are the fundamental data basis for marketing departments to measure their program's effectiveness and their campaigns holistically. Surveys not only allow complete focus on pure success metrics, but it also allows creativity, innovation, and product feedback — all of which can be incorporated into this process.

Impact

- Panels, surveys, and target group interviews provide good, solid customer feedback on product usage, innovations, and trial and awareness insights that help to optimize both the product and marketing campaign effectiveness.
- Solid customer feedback helps to optimize personalization, recommendation, and advertising strategies; this will result in higher conversions in future campaigns and journeys.

Fields of Actions

- Design and implement a market research organization, process, and platform.
- Align the market research with the marketing campaign planning and analytics (data model, timings, etc).

IT Support and Platforms

- Market intelligence (survey) platforms.
- Experience feedback platforms.

M14 CONNECT SALES

In our Gedankenexperiment 2.0, we discussed the need for a central profile database; most of the described ma.tomics also reference data management and customer data platform that, when used, can implement a customer 360 profile view. These kinds of multi-channel engagement suites also raise a challenge in the organizational domain. Historically, marketing, sales, commerce, services, production, and backend are isolated teams. In a perfect world, we would reorganize them and surround our customers with perfect experiences. However, from a leadership perspective, we build huge matrix organizations that can't be easily managed and controlled. In terms of challenges from math-men marketing, the most critical interface I've seen in most organizations was the alignment between marketing, sales, and often on top: commerce.

In most cases, there is some kind of competition or, even worse, resentment between these teams that is real. While the marketing team claims to open the funnel and bring people into the brand's universe, the sales team counter argues that the money is earned in their territory. From a marketing point of view, we need to know how to overcome this skirmish. To be data-driven means to attribute what you're doing entirely against the final success measurement. This is in all of the business models I've seen and at the end of those models was an increase in sales! For this reason, to help other businesses, I've defined this ma.tomic group, which includes the two important sub-topics of marketing mix modeling and trade promotion management. Although, there might be an overlap with the ma.tomics M8.5 and M8.6 from the chapter about PEO activation mix; while M8 deals with the fact of activation mix it includes media mix and trade promotion optimization. This ma.tomic focuses more on the organizational and IT challenger to include sales and service, to set up a working model and infrastructure for marketing mix modeling, and joined trade promotion management together with the sales team.

M14.1 Marketing Mix Modelling — Incremental Sales Uplifts

While ma.tomic M8 deals with the optimization against different success measures in your different funnel layers, there is a much higher cruising altitude to gain insights on possible optimizations and waste. The marketing universe is full rich of data, but it isn't just that — there is more to it than that, including the pool of sales data. Similar to our known data lake, it is here we can access an entire universe of data describing the complete sales process hopefully in an enterprise-wide aligned taxonomy.

As a marketer, the most powerful data are the incremental ups and downs of sales revenues. Just in case we can slice and dice them in the dimensions of sold products or SKUs, locations, etc, we can compare the actions we take against the effects in the sales universe. Correlations on timeframes can be used to attribute sales success to marketing activations.

However, you must be cautious; what every data scientist learns within his first lessons is that there is a huge difference between causation and correlations (Wikipedia, 2021). Correlations just mean that there are two times the same pattern on a time-related measure. Prominent examples are cited all over the internet, though for me, one of the funniest is that the more milk is processed to cheese in Switzerland, the more roses are imported into Germany.

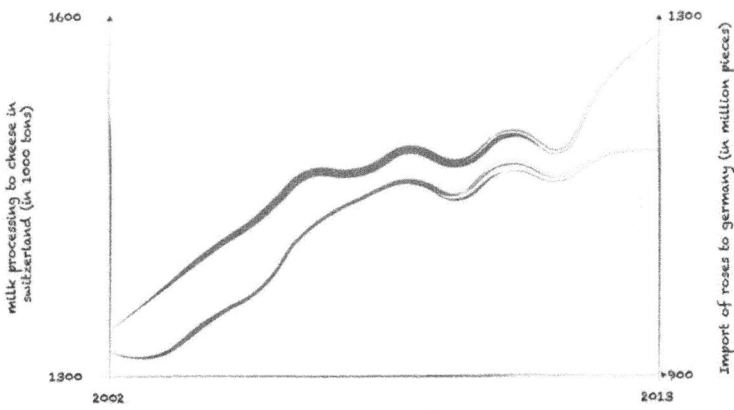

If it is implemented in the right way, the correlation between sales uplifts and marketing activations is a very powerful tool. Marketing mix modeling (MMM) algorithms allow us to attribute sales success on time dimensions and geo-locations, with the spending on marketing programs, campaigns, and journeys. The MMM result provides a comprehensive view of the joined sales and marketing universe and correlations within this space.

Impact

- Marketing mix modeling models and the integration of further sales data optimizes the marketing spendings, not only in single programs and campaigns but the comprehensive overarching insights as well, which allow us to optimize explicitly against the sales net revenue.

Fields of Actions

- Align the marketing taxonomy with the sales taxonomy.
- Measure incremental sales up-/down-turns and correlate them towards your marketing activations.
- Design and implement a marketing mix modeling algorithm.

IT Support and Platforms

- Master Data Management and Governance Platforms
- Marketing Mix Modelling Platforms

M14.2 Trade Promotion Effects and Pricing

In the intro to this ma.tomic group, I've referenced the often-seen rivalry between marketing and sales. One root cause of this I believe is that there is also marketing in the sales departments, which is something that I have witnessed myself. While it is labeled as trade promotions and pricing, it is still part of the 4Ps of the marketing mix (price, promotion, place, product). The marketing within the sales department is a core driver for higher volumes and better margins. So, aside from the access to the sales data, there is also the need for organizational alignment with our colleagues from the sales team. The trade promotions (TPM) field of action has to be considered in each data-driven marketing architecture as otherwise, success measures may be seen in a wrong interpretation regarding the cause-effect chain. Be sure to remember my short excursion into the world of causation and correlation above. Trade promotions like discounts, volume rebates, direct sales merchandising have a huge effect on the sales volumes and figures. Predictive pricing models help to find the best discount and sales volume ratio to maximize the return on investment.

This ma.tomic deals with the set up of a joined, overarching target operating model that includes the two pillars of data-driven pricing and trade promotion management which is somewhere in-between the marketing and sales universe.

Impact

- An overarching operating model for trade promotion management helps to balance budgeting planning on the most promising goals in sales *and* marketing.

Fields of Actions

- Align the sales and marketing organization and set up comprehensive planning processes including both the marketing activations and the trade promotions.
- Design and Implement trade promotion models and dashboards within the marketing reporting.

IT Support and Platforms

- Trade promotion management platforms.

M15 STAY LEAN AND SHARE — SMART KPIs

By now, we have gone through fundamental ma.tomics like carbon, hydrogen, and oxygen in the real world. Nothing would exist without these fundamental atoms; most of the solid states in the world are built out of at least one of them. This is similar to our first ma.tomic groups for the marketing universe, taxonomy and agile, etc. which are then followed by the more operative ones about PEO optimization, the flow of actions and journeys, and time dependencies. We have seen some exotic ones like the cross-device and platform ma.tomic.

With the last ma.tomic group, we entered the world of measuring essential reach, success, and sales data to have a look at how we can close the loop for intelligent data-driven marketing. This is our entry door towards the last galaxy of data & analytics. I will start with some kind of mandatory pre-work that is more related to change management and the way we behave when working with data in an enterprise environment. This will be followed by more ma.tomics dealing with the target operating model for data & analytics and predictive algorithms.

M15.1 Stay Lean: Measures, KPIs, and Dimensions

There was a discussion I had once with a client in the middle of his data-driven marketing initiative. In his marketing technology stack, he used endless amounts of different specialized platforms; the huge usage of his big data platforms resulted in myriads of unaligned dashboards that showed different KPIs and dimensions. This all resulted in him having mountains of data but no real insights. He was excited by my idea of getting lean, but the initial approach of cutting 80% of the dashboard budgets and focussing only on a core set was a starting point. However, it isn't what "stay lean" claims in this ma.tomic. We had some back and forth conversations about the definition of lean and how to implement this properly after that.

If we look at the Lean and Kanban theory, the two essential capabilities are first to cut waste, and second, to organize your production so that all necessary parts are just one arms-length away in every production step. This is what we also need to guarantee; from my point of view, this means cutting dashboards is not the golden path that you must take. The best way to get lean in data and analytics is to establish some kind of mining the right data at the right spots, purify these core measures in essential

KPIs, and deliver them to the people in the organizations that translate the KPIs into a competitive advantage and business results.

The second ma.tomic group has shown us that every data-driven marketing initiative has to define a core taxonomy and set up governance to provide an essential set of KPIs and dimensions to optimize the marketing performance. Lean data-driven marketing models focus on the fundamental measures we learned in our Gedankenexperiment 2.0: Reach, reach1+, the universe, actions, budget, and customer satisfaction (NPS). Based on the measures we can calculate nearly every marketing KPI.

Lean also means to use the taxonomy as the meta-model for your data lake. The mined data need to be purified in easy to read dashboards and delivered into the organization in an "easy to consume" way. This is often only one or two KPIs so the dashboard isn't being overwhelmed and showing too much information. As aforementioned previously, the right information is always one arm's length away!

Implementing this ma.tomic means to master the challenge to implement a data mining of the fundamental set of measures in all touchpoints, channels, customer journeys, and dimensions instead of blowing up the dashboards with highly sophisticated KPIs and algorithms. We have seen the technical challenge of measuring reach and success, so now we need to balance this with the organizational need for different KPIs to pursue the business in a highly competitive way.

Impact

- Lean data-driven models save time when finding the correct information.
- Providing the essential information but not more at the right moment in time helps to stay focussed on your business goals instead of wasting budget on non-performing dashboards nobody understands and uses.

Fields of Actions

- Establish data-driven culture and skills on how to work with dimensions, measures, and KPIs in your enterprise-wide taxonomy.
- Find out what the perfect set of information is that different roles need to pursue their business within all their different process

steps. Reduce the marketing information to an absolute minimum and guarantee to mine core measures consistently in all touchpoints.

IT Support and Platforms

- ETL and analytics platforms.
- Master data management and governance platforms.

M15.2 Share Your Data Assets: The New Imperative

The ma.tomics we have seen deal with the best target operating model and technology to set up a high-performing marketing machine. Though, we've also seen we need to work on the skills and capabilities of all people involved so we can bring them up to speed in our new marketing universe. However, there is one thing more we need to consider: the behavior of these people in our transition towards an intelligent data-driven enterprise. It becomes more obvious that with the endless amounts of data that are generated every day in modern enterprise organizations, there is a counter-trend on the horizon. People start protecting their data pools and assets because this gives them the right to exist further within the company organization and processes. So instead of sharing data, taxonomies, and insights, the opposite effect evolves by hiding and protecting the proprietary data structure and attributes. Sharing in these cases is only done through aggregated insights to pre-defined counter-parts.

All the taxonomies, lean information management, and enterprise-wide data lakes only work if everybody acts in the same way by sharing data assets. This topic needs to be addressed and as a result, a new way of open data sharing culture aligned with a corporate data protection strategy has to be implemented — this would be a ma.tomic that deals with a new imperative within your marketing workforce.

Impact

- Shared data sources instead of shared aggregated insights allow us to build overarching data models and algorithms. This helps to eliminate the shortsighted focus on isolated actions and instead, focus on the comprehensive way of doing marketing.
- Sharing stimulates creativity and collaboration; this will end-up creating faster innovation cycles and generated unexpected insights.

Fields of Actions

- Establish a data-driven culture and sharing imperative.
- Design and implement open data architectures across the organization.
- Design and implement a data supply chain and governance processes.

IT Support and Platforms

- Collaborative sharing platforms and intranets.

M16 EXPLORATIVE REPORTING AND DATA SCIENCE

Up until now, we have touched upon the subjects of the necessary behavioral change to share data and to carefully balance the demand for data in a lean data-driven marketing setup. Therefore, it's time to have a look at the ma.tomic group for the high performing target operating model for the data and analytics galaxy. Apart from the lean approach, I've seen the most successful brands using a threefold approach to cover all needs out of the organization. First, the one we all know the best and also tie towards analytics is the use of standard reporting. On-demand or within fixed frequencies, there are different kinds of roles in an organization that can consume a fixed dashboard or PDF with various KPIs split by different dimensions. The most prominent representatives of these reports are overviews on reach and channels, web analytics in the form of visits, likes, shares, or budget plan/actual comparisons.

With the advent of explorative and collaborative data analytics platforms, the fixed report has been partly replaced by fixed data cubes that can be used with a more questing attitude. The data cubes follow the enterprise-wide taxonomy and allow the building of stories on demand, which would be based on the current demand and questions in different marketing departments. The access is still the same; while in the first case, the user pulls or gets pushed fixed reports, he can do the same with data cubes (sources) in the more explorative second case.

This differs when it comes to the third case we will see in this ma.tomic group: the use of data science. Here we need to steer away from our known, common approach of consuming data and reports. Instead, we need to learn to postulate a hypothesis and forward this on to a data scientist. He is the one digging into the data to find confirmation or maybe also proof that we have thought in the wrong direction. 100% data-driven based on algorithms and not influenced by gut decisions whatsoever.

M16.1 Get the Basics: Standard Reporting

Classic, standard reporting is an essential part to close the loop of strategic marketing planning, preparation, execution, and analytics. You can compare this to driving a race car; there is a need to have some basic KPIs available on a fixed frequency or in real-time. We need to know the fuel level, speed, and RPMs. The team will consume more data like the tire pressure, motor heat, etc. in the back for us. The insights are frequently shared with each report close to the data-driven loop. Without knowing the solid baseline and incremental enhancements, the basis for any next iteration of strategic planning and optimization is not given.

For that reason, a comprehensive set of standard reports builds the elementary oil for daily data-driven operations. Also part of this ma.tomic is to think about the way you'd like to distribute this information. At this stage, remember our paradigm of "each information is just one arm-length away." There are plenty of ways to distribute this information: via self-service in a portal, via pushed standard mailings and newsletters, by voice request, or as real-time dashboards in open spaces — and this is to just name a few examples. In combination with an enterprise-wide style guide for data presentations and the use of charts, this is an extremely powerful way of staying on top of your data and translating insights into a competitive advantage. Do not think too much time about necessary filters, the slice and dice options, and other sophisticated ways of digging into details. The main focus is on sharing basic information across the marketing organization via different communication channels. All the rest is part of the next ma.tomics.

Impact

- Data-driven marketing relies on the principles of agile and incremental optimizations. Without fixed and lean reporting that allows regular tracking of the reached success, ongoing optimizations are not possible.

Fields of Actions

- Design and implement a reporting framework and corporate design principles
- Reduce the bunch on marketing reports to the absolute minimum and guarantee to share them across the organization via multiple distributions (voice, dashboards, email reports, live screens, etc.).

IT Support and Platforms

- Collaborative reporting platforms.

M16.2 Explorative Insights

With the advent of data and analytics platforms that allow to slice and dice data cubes and to collaboratively work on stories a new era evolved, the pure distribution of fixed sets of data and reports that were the focus is no longer. Instead, the systems allow us to share data in a fixed taxonomy and the people in front of their user interfaces are digging into the details on their own. This means these platforms allow to build of many tables and charts with sophisticated filters, parameters, and calculated expressions. These insights can be combined in a story that can be shared via collaborative workflows and communities.

But what does this mean for us as a CMO or marketing manager that is responsible for setting up intelligent data-driven marketing? The biggest challenge here and focus of this ma.tomic is to enable your organization to take advantage of this new way of working with data.

The essence of successful explorative insights I've seen within leading brands has been the investment in two major pillars. The first the organizational model has been enhanced. Following the idea of data supply chain management, each department needs to set up roles that allow to mine, purify and translate data into action.

The second is to lift the maturity level of your whole organization and processes so you can work with explorative insights. This means you should have a clear IT strategy for a collaborative and explorative data and analytics platform and the enablement of your workforce on how to use this in an impactful way.

Impact

- The swarm intelligence by enabling the organization to filter, slice, and dice data cubes stimulates creativity within the teams and finally will end up in a broader set of insights and optimizations for better marketing.
- The new collaborative way of working with insights and sharing across the organization helps to combine different points of view. This will leverage your data asset and is going to transform insights into a competitive advantage.

Fields of Actions

- Enhance your target operating model with roles to mine, purify, and translate data into a competitive advantage which is based on the idea of a data supply chain.
- Design and implement an IT strategy for a collaborative and explorative data and analytics platform.
- Ensure your organization knows how to use explorative insights via training and to establish a data-driven culture of sharing insights.

IT Support and Platforms

- Collaborative and explorative data and analytics platforms.
- IT strategy on explorative data management.

M16.3 Working Data Science

While we have seen a new explorative and collaborative way of working with data, it is still a similar setup to the one we have learned in the past, which is by sharing fixed reports. We are now opening the ma.tomic of data science that includes a new way of working with data. No longer is every single individual of the organization working on solely the data. Instead, there will be a small team of scientists dedicated to working exclusively on the raw data and lake, all the rest just postulates a business hypothesis. So, where is the difference? In the previous ma.tomics, people know the structure and content of their reports or at least, are trained on the corporate data taxonomy to harvest insights via explorative data management. With this ma.tomic, however, we're moving away from this approach. Now, people don't know the details about the full scope of data that is included in their data lake because it would be far too complex to train the entire organization to stay on top of all the data points.

Instead, a small, central group takes care of huge mountains of data and gets enabled with special tools and platforms to dig into the insights hidden in this endless universe of data. For most marketing departments this is a new way of working with data, so they must implement it, which means they have to incubate a central data science team and workflow so they can integrate them in their target operating model for data and analytics. You must be aware that this group requires a special set of tools and platforms so they can properly do their jobs.

In addition to the organizational phase-in of new digital talents like data scientists, architects, and analysts it also includes new processes for the operational marketing team. They need to learn how to postulate a hypothesis, how to forward and discuss this with the data science team, and finally, how to manage the answers of that scientist team to transform big data into smart insights, optimizations, and recommendations.

Working data science is the organizational and skill setup of a central team first by finding the right talents, and secondly, the process integration into the daily work of a marketing department. Different organizational approaches need to be considered to locate the data science competence within several departments (e.g. marketing, IT, and finance). In most cases I've seen, they were centrally steered within the headquarter or a tiny set of regional hub spots.

Impact

- Process and organizational data science integration allow you to gain the maximum insights and optimizations out of your enterprise-wide data assets.
- The focus and global use of a small team of specialist save costs and increase the efficiency in transforming data into insights and competitive advantage

Fields of Actions

- Design and implement a target operating model for data science (process and team), including a workflow to forward hypothesis to a central working team.
- Enable your data science team with the necessary sophisticated data and analytics platforms.

IT Support and Platforms

- Data lake platforms.
- Sophisticated data science platforms.
- Workflow platforms to integrate the team in the marketing organization.

M17 PREDICT THE FUTURE

When I began my education at John Hopkins Online University for "the data scientists toolbox," two of the fundamental elements excited me on the course. The first was the correlation and causality topics I've mentioned above, where Swiss cheese production correlates with the import of roses in Germany; between the two topics, it's clear that there's no causality. The second is quite easy to understand but it was the most powerful concept; the maturity levels of working with data, starting with pure descriptive models and reports, and from there stepping up the ladder via diagnostics (the why), predictive (what will happen), and then the final level of prescriptive (what you do).

If we trust in this development, we need to invest more and more in programmatically driven optimizations. I've only seen a few of my clients passing the descriptive or diagnostic level towards a more predictive closed-loop marketing target operating model. Therefore, please ask yourself: are you still looking at reach, GRPs, and conversions in your journey? What we all want to reach is this predictive level where an algorithm tells us to start better on a Tuesday evening with red instead of blue creatives via a sequence of activation (A, C, C, D, E) to reach a minimum conversion of x%. For that reason, we close our data and analytics section with the ma.tomic group that can enhance your maturity and head you in the direction of a predictive universe.

M17.1 Programmatic Program and Campaign Planning

Years ago, I was asked to speak at a marketing summit and it was at the time of the advent of data management platforms and the power of programmatic advertising. For most of the CMOs, this was a black box as only a few sophisticated agencies knew the details.

I started the presentation with the claim: "a tattoo appears differently, depending on the person who looks at it — welcome to the programmatic world in a predictive universe." Now, years later as I'm writing this book, I have to admit that this is still true; that claim is the holy grail of intelligent data-driven marketing. We have seen in the ma.tomic about Newton's law of action equals reaction that we can build a reverse funnel, starting upside down with the final goal we'd like to reach and from there, going up the funnel to see what is necessary to reach the desired actions in the upper funnel levels. Let's develop this idea a bit further now by bringing in data science and predictive algorithms. In a nearly perfect data-driven world, there must be a way where we no longer spread the budget across programs and campaigns at the beginning of our next marketing cycle. Instead, the definition of the pursuit outcomes that build the starting point for the predictive models, trimmed by historic data to calculate the overall budget, audiences, journeys, marketing assets, and actions to reach these goals.

So this ma.tomic is a big one; no longer do we use descriptive and diagnostic insights in our data to prepare the next marketing cycle. We connect predictive algorithms with a programmatic way of planning and execution so we can achieve a fully automated closed-loop marketing.

Impact

- Predictive planning in combination with programmatic execution and automation eliminates the human factor and leverages the full potential of intelligent data-driven marketing.
- All of the conversion optimizations are highly efficient and fully supported by machine learning and predictive algorithms.

Fields of Actions

- Implement machine learning not only with single touchpoints; instead, use algorithms to optimize the full flow of actions through the entire funnel and journey.
- Use predictive algorithms to predict the most successful optimizations for your next marketing planning cycle.

IT Support and Platforms

- None, because this is all about orchestrating existing technology.

M17.2 Next Best Action

With the advent of programmatic advertising, we have seen a shift in the way machine learning and algorithms are used. In the early days, we collected millions of data points to run different analyses to find out the most promising channel mix and audiences. However, this has changed. In a universe where we have understood our funnel and journeys by action and reaction chains and can slice and dice our data cubes by hundreds of dimension like creatives, campaigns, regions, etc, we can enhance the concept of pure massively scaled A/B testing by using predictive next best action algorithms. The next best action combines the isolated disciplines of look-a-like modeling for finding the best-performing audiences and propensity scoring for recommending a product, next call to action, or personalization of the current touchpoint. High sophisticated algorithms are mixing all these previously isolated algorithms to make one big programmatic optimization.

A good example is the targeting options that social networks provide; they were well-known for their granular ways of addressing audiences at the start, though with more advanced ad formats, targeting algorithms, etc. it is clear that the best approach is to target a maximum on the region and a few high-level attributes and trust into the technology and math behind. The machine finds the best converting people by highly complex propensity and optimization algorithms. Let the machines do their work; machines much better in comparison to humans, and what we do with our brains and gut feelings.

Journeys through our funnels become more complex; often, we have dozens of ways in parallel people can pass the next conversion layer. people will bounce out of one journey to enter a new one.

We learned in the ma.tomics about the PEO optimization that there is a need for real-time interaction monitoring and optimization; in comparison,t his ma.tomic focuses on interactions between different journeys and how to push people back into a journey or transfer them if the scores show higher propensities.

Mastering the ma.tomic of next best action means relying on a fully programmatic closed-loop marketing from planning, via preparation and execution towards data and analytics supported by predictive algorithms. Therefore, the focus was no longer the single optimization of a touchpoint, but the cross journey optimization in every touchpoint.

Impact

- The power of data can be used to optimize cross journeys and your overall marketing planning and execution to generate the highest conversions.

Fields of Actions

- Use predictive propensity scorings and the next best action algorithms end-to-end in your marketing target operating model (IT and process level).

IT Support and Platforms

- None, because this is about orchestrating existing technology in the best way.

M17.3 Text, Image, and Voice Recognition

Using technology for predictive actions includes another special discipline, and the entry to a huge number of these algorithms is the customer's voice. For this reason, the machine needs to "understand" what he is talking about. Therefore, this section covers information on the ability of your marketing technology stack to translate the customer's interactions into data and insights.

There are three fundamental ways of interactions: text messages, voice, and image/video postings. Modern text, image, and voice recognition algorithms detect if product logos or brands are shown in a posted picture or video, blog, etc. It also measures the related word of mouth and Net Promoter Score (NPS) values. This kind of "digital public listening" of text, images, videos, and voices enables access to market feedback in real-time without any influence on the panel group by survey questions.

Impact

- Using text, image, and voice recognition algorithms enhances the classic ways for market and customer feedback loops. This broadens the input attributes for your predictive scores and by that the conversion propensity.

Fields of Actions

- Design and implement text, voice, and image recognition frameworks on all bi-directional customer interaction touchpoints (e.g. bots, social networks, in-/outbound calls, etc).

IT Support and Platforms

- Text, voice, image, and video recognition frameworks.

M18 THERE IS ONE LAST THING — CREATIVITY

The first version of my ma.tomic framework contained only 17, and this one was missed, so I decided to add it now. We have seen in the chapter about using physics in marketing that the light speed in marketing is not data, it is creativity!

What would marketing be without the warm feelings when Coca Cola's truck comes around the virtual TV corner decorated with millions of lights, without the shocking moments of Benetton's ads, the sweet fun of Red Bull comic heroes getting wings, without someone who tells us that we can just do it, without a man with a cigarette riding a horse, without billions of people waiting for the Superbowl ad breaks, and millions more cool and creative ways of burning a message into our brains.

Everyone has hundreds of these exceptional stories and brands in mind and it also demonstrates that intelligent data-driven marketing is not the end of agencies. Creativity is still the winning factor in this game; while technology has pushed us into a math-men world, but we, as a human, still react and feel like we have done this in the mad-men world. Everyone likes and recognizes iconic epic brands. Therefore, I added this ma.tomic to honor the fact that creativity is the mystic power behind successful marketing, aside from all the data-driven ways of tuning our high performing marketing machines.

M18.1 Engage With Your Audience — Creativity is King

Even the best working models and organizations based on data and automated IT platforms don't perform if there is no creativity; in other words, a high-performing marketing machine fed with standard activations will generate a large number of boring customer experiences. For that reason, creativity is still the light speed in marketing, where all other things need to be measured relatively against. The Old Spice man has shown all of us how to revitalize a dead dog by combining data, technology, budget, and creativity; meanwhile, the "The Man Your Man Could Smell Like" campaign garnered some incredible statistics as it skyrocketed in pop culture (Fernandez, 2011).

Key statistics of that campaign include:

- On Day 1, the campaign received 5.9 million YouTube views, more than Obama's victory speech after 24 hours (source: Visible Measures).
- On Day 2, Old Spice had 8 out of the top 11 most popular videos on the web (source: Visible Measures).
- By Day 3, the campaign eclipsed 20 million YouTube views.
- One week post-launch, the work had been watched more than 40 million times.
- Twitter followers increased by 2700%.
- Facebook fan interactions went up 800%
- Facebook fans increased by 60% (from 500,000 to 800,000).
- Oldspice.com traffic increased 300%.
- YouTube subscribers for the brand more than doubled, increasing from 65,000 to 150,000.
- Old Spice also became the #1 All-Time Most Viewed and #2 Most Subscribed Branded Channel on YouTube.

For now, that's the end of explaining that ma.tomic; now we venture to early 1965, a time at which Don Draper, the legendary ad man, is facing a meltdown. His agency's clients are deserting, the partners are squabbling, and Adland has got wind that Sterling Cooper Draper Price is in trouble. At the time, Don has returned from a demotivating meeting with Heinz, which was a meeting that he hoped could bring his agency back on track. Unfortunately, the prospect rebuffed him, saying he wanted to wait and see "if you're still in business in six months." Peggy, his trusted copywriter, asks Don, "What are we going to do?" He said: "We're creative. We're gonna sit at our desks typing while the walls fall around us because we're the least important, most important thing there is."

Impact

- Without creativity in marketing, there is no real customer experience.
- Real engagement comes from natural curiosity stimulated by the creativity of each customer communication.

Fields of Actions

- Carefully balance the change towards a data-driven culture and preserve the high importance of creative customer activations.

M18.2 Create Emotions — Storytelling and Purposeful Marketing

With the advent of moving away from purely paid activations to a more balanced paid, owned, and earned approach we see the fact that content is king. Whether we name it storytelling, customer experience management, purposeful, or green marketing, etc. it is still selling the story around your product. It's at this last moment when Leonardo DiCaprio, who played Jordan Belford in Wolf of Wall Street, asks one of his seminar visitors: "Please sell me this pen. The moment you start talking about the pen you have lost. You need to ask questions; you should put the answers into context and design a story around it. This is what people will attract and what they will remember."

There is no need to write any more about the subject of storytelling in marketing as everybody universally agrees that this is the best way. But why have we not seen that many brands implementing this the right way? I've seen most brands relying on the classic product-driven approach. My educated guess is that it sounds easy but implementing a consistent end-to-end storytelling approach in a bigger enterprise is a huge cultural change and the outcome is unknown — maybe data and short sprints will help this.

Trust me, you must follow the paradigm "creativity is the lightspeed" and implement the rest of over 50 ma.tomics to reach the math-men world — the combination of creative storytelling and intelligent data-driven target operating models is the winning approach.

mpact

- People prefer and buy stories and not products.
- Good storytelling will strengthen the brand, which will end up in higher financial margins.

ields of Actions

- Establish storytelling and high-end content production process.

From Mad-Men to Math-Men Marketing

Imagine New York in the 1960s. Don Draper has just said, "People tell you who they are, but we ignore it because we want them to be who we want them to be." As a marketer, your clients are always telling you about themselves. Don is quite wise in this regard, even though he is unaware of how much his world will change. The Math-Men of the 20th century will stick to this paradigm half a century later in a way he hadn't foreseen. With each visit and click on a website, like, share, or tweet, customers tell us insightful information you can't afford to ignore. The new challenge is that there are mountains of data and you must dig to its inner core to mine and purify the ones you should pay attention to and ignore the white noise.

In the 1960s on Madison Avenue in New York, a brilliant marketer might have put up a billboard or launched a print campaign in the hopes to see sales improve. Today in 2020, where we all pursue hyper-accurate targeting, 1:1 personalization, and AI-driven recommendations, it is no longer defined by mad-men guesswork. A new universe of intelligent data-driven marketing led by the math-men is in place and has changed Don's microcosmos fundamentally.

This old mad-men universe is like looking at the TV in two-dimensional black and white videos with an isolated focus on creativity and final sales profits. Customer-centric math-men marketing possesses a deep, multi-dimensional understanding of who your customers are, how they behave within hundreds of journeys, and what motivates them to love your brand and to buy your products.

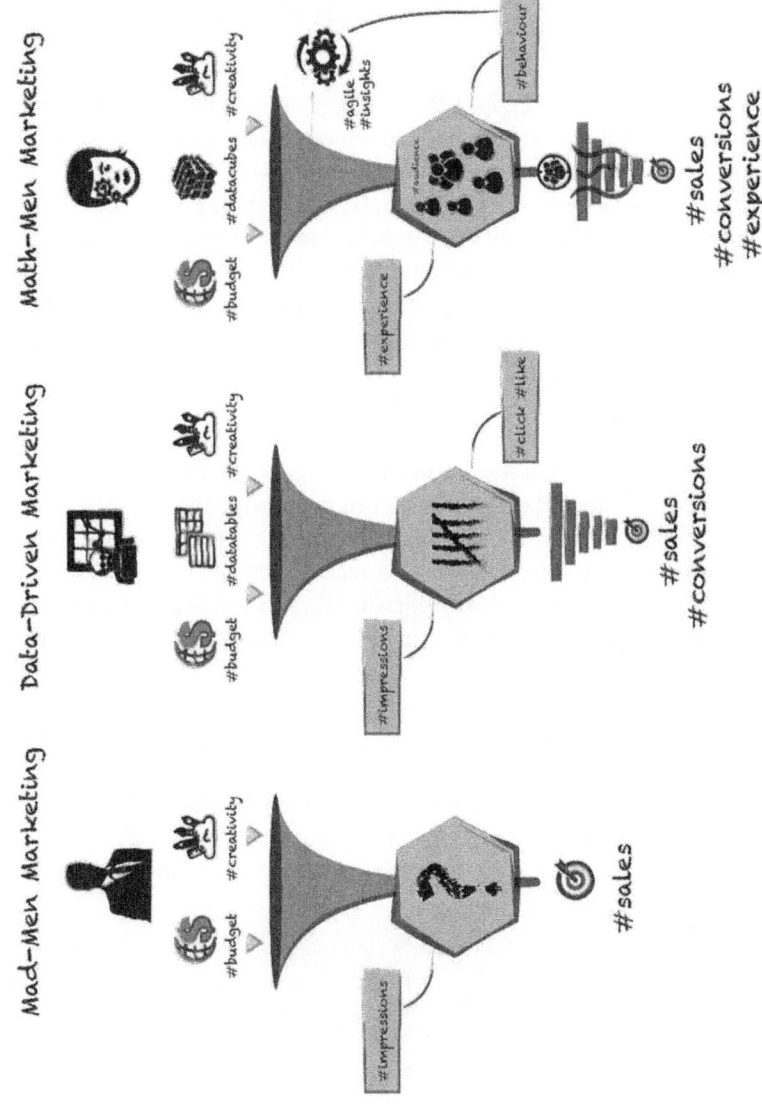

This also means we can say goodbye to another brilliant marketing sageness. "Half the money I spend on advertising is wasted; the trouble is I don't know which half." This famous quote from a successful US merchant and forefather of marketing, John Wanamaker, was uttered over 100 years ago now. Guiding customers via journeys through our owned ecosystem and using campaigns to fill this funnel and avoid people bouncing out allows us to triple the marketing efficiency. This means we can no longer flip a coin and hope to pick the right half. Data, algorithms, and an agile target operating model allow us to permanently increase our insights and by that the desired actions and results of our marketing efforts.

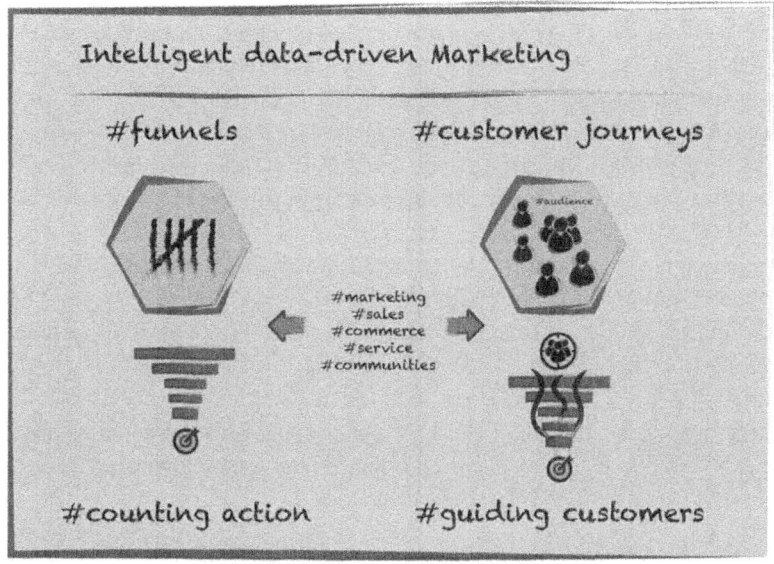

Sadly many companies remain in the mad-men universe, burning money by only investing in reach and creativity. As competition increased, there is a need to stop treating your marketing department as a cost center. It's the starting point of each customer journey and the ultimate fuel for running your business model with maximum performance.

We have now seen the easiness of the marketing initial frame of reference by just throwing a few balls on a defined audience, followed by some physical laws and more than 50 tiny ma.tomics, each focussing on necessary capabilities. It's time to share a final view on the way how to transform your existing operating model towards a high performing marketing machine.

In my opening chapter to this book, I spoke about applying business engineering to marketing. Once, I explained to one of my clients that business engineering is the artwork of replacing the engine of a plane while flying across the ocean. You can't stop business execution to draw a new blueprint of how you'd like to run your business in the future to then restart and follow this new innovative setup.

Instead, you need to cautiously change your current operating model piece by piece. We have learned in previous chapters about more physics in marketing that we need to eliminate waste and impediments to reach a perfect flow — that we need to balance the power of new energy we bring into a new system to avoid our harmonic oscillation levels out too long on the new plateau. Without new energy, the chaos measured as entropy will increase and destroy every well-designed operating model. But how should our math-men universe look like? Is there a general structure of our solid-state "intelligent data-driven marketing" besides the gravity waves and ma.tomics we've seen in the second part of this book?

I'm still a fan of comparing an organization with a pipe system, which is where liquid in form of campaigns and journeys are pushed through. The specific setup of such an agile closed-loop cycle out of our 50 ma.tomics we call the operating model — it's great that the first five letters of our ma.tomics build the word ma.tom which can be read as "marketing agile target operating model." In one of my biggest data-driven marketing transformation programs, I once sketched this closed-loop cycle to explain the main process on a single canvas.

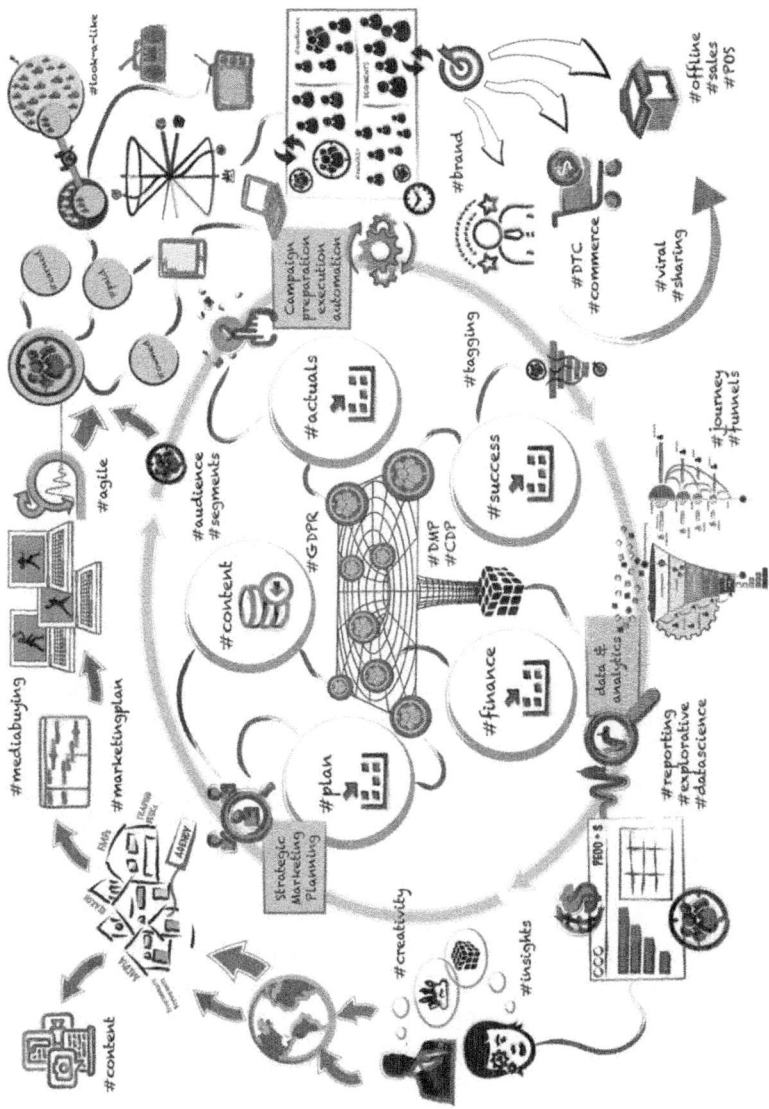

This explains a closed and infinite loop, so it doesn't matter where we start explaining the main parts of this operating model. Let's start at the left middle of the cycle, where a CMO is looking for new prospects and customers. The idea he has in mind needs to be translated into a vision and goals. This briefing has then circled the world and translated by the teams involved in a working marketing plan. Besides the budget, goals, strategic audiences, and planned activation mix, the plan also generates a demand for the necessary marketing assets (creatives, communications, etc.).

Once the plan is finalized, dedicated campaigns are added in an agile backlog, and prepared and activated in the myriads of paid, owned, and earned pipelines to reach the customer. In case he or she is attracted, the reaction is three-fold. The customer becomes aware of the brand, product, or service, they then interact with the brand in a direct-to-customer scenario (e.g. a newsletter subscription), or lastly, he is using one of our offline points of sale to inform him to buy the products. As we live in a connected, social world, we hope that we attracted a real fan that is willing to share their interest in our brand via social networks.

Through this round trip, we mine different types of data on three main islands. Starting with our program and campaign structure, this first island includes all of the planned values. Delving further, we see all the actual data representing our reach and frequency in the paid, owned, and earned ecosystem. The island of what we measure as success can be an increase in the brand value, a direct action, offline purchases in one of our stores, or triggered by our field sales team.

All these mountains of data are now used to close the loop of intelligent data-driven marketing. To do this, we purify them into a standard report showing our fundamental KPIs of the few measures we can quantify. Or, we provide them in a fixed taxonomy within pre-defined data cubes. Last but not least, our data science team has access to all of the data to answer our hypothesis. This is your main marketing universe for the "closed-loop" process of design math-men marketing set up to run fast and also fail fast.

The main focus areas to design such an operating model are the ability to build unique profiles and segmentation to use them in your funnel and journey management. Driven by demand windows and taking care of the time dimension and in line with all privacy constraints. This ability is based on the fundaments of a cloud-based technology stack and data management that provides comprehensive end-to-end data and analytics. This allows us to use the hyper-accurate target audiences in the three main epics of advertisements & retargeting, personalization, and next best action recommendations.

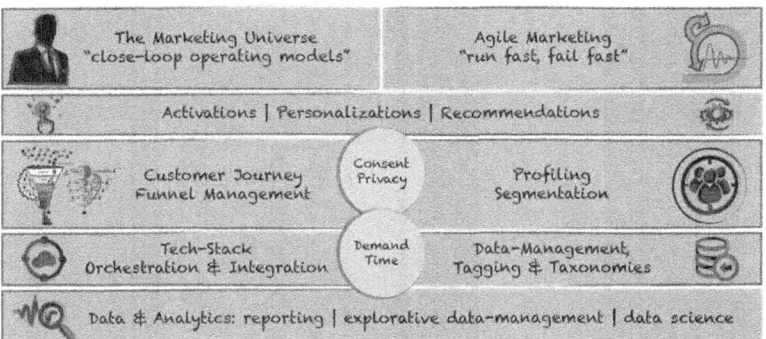

This can be reached by applying the ma.tomics in a transformation program. It's the best results I've seen in programs that implemented the framework with ongoing improvement. Instead of using them to design a final blueprint, we always used them as some kind of backlog epics that has to be refined in stories that can be implemented within 5–10 working days. This fits the idea that "everything is in motion" and Isaac Newton's law of action equals reaction. The harmonic oscillator has shown us that the more energy is pumped into an existing ecosystem, the higher and longer the sinus amplitude swings around our desired new baseline.

This is the congeniality of the ma.tomic framework. Just take these melanges out of small and big atoms to build your solid-state of intelligent data-driven marketing. If there would be perfect blueprints of what and how to implement anyhow, all companies would run in the same direction. But a competitive advantage is something your competitors can't copy and implement easily. It takes you apart from them and allows you to run better math-men marketing. This also means to detach yourself from the stereotype that the transition from mad-men to math-men is an isolated IT workstream or a strategy program within your business department. Only a mixed team of skilled IT nerds, thrilled marketing enthusiasts, and experienced experts can transform your current way of doing marketing to be 100% data-driven.

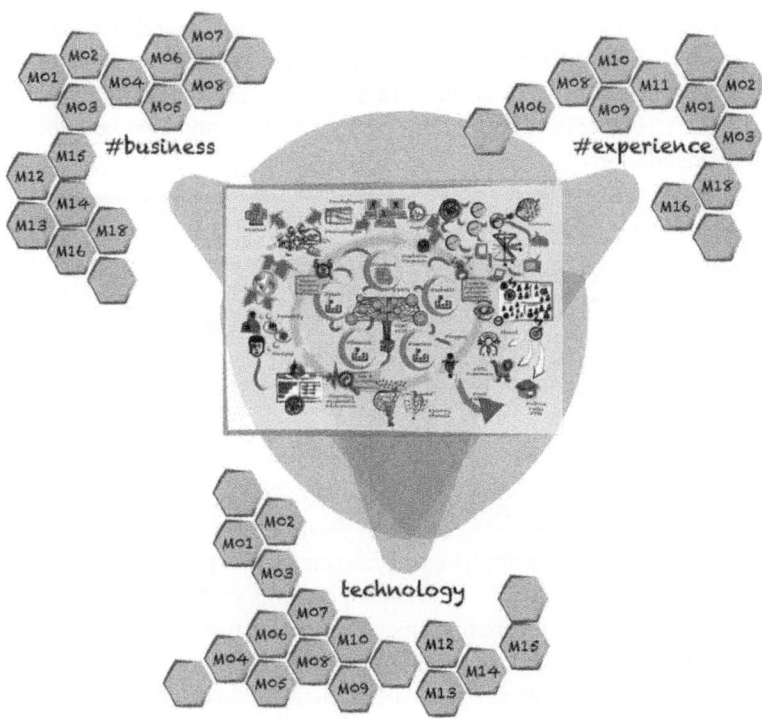

Over the last 23 years, I've learned that there are some fundamental milestones you need to encounter on your way to successfully do math-men marketing. The starting point is the mad-men baseline, which is fully focussed on creativity and budget and zero insights by mining marketing data. The first maturity state "growth hacking" is to master the closed loop on a process level for all paid, owned, and earned touchpoints, while still relying on a more context and funnel-driven architecture. From there, we can improve the way we work to the state of "customer-centric data-driven marketing." Here, we put the audience in the middle of all activations and improve our funnel with personalized journeys. This is the champions league, so from here, special improvements like pricing and brand valuation might be your next evolution.

From Mad-Men to Math-Men Marketing   217

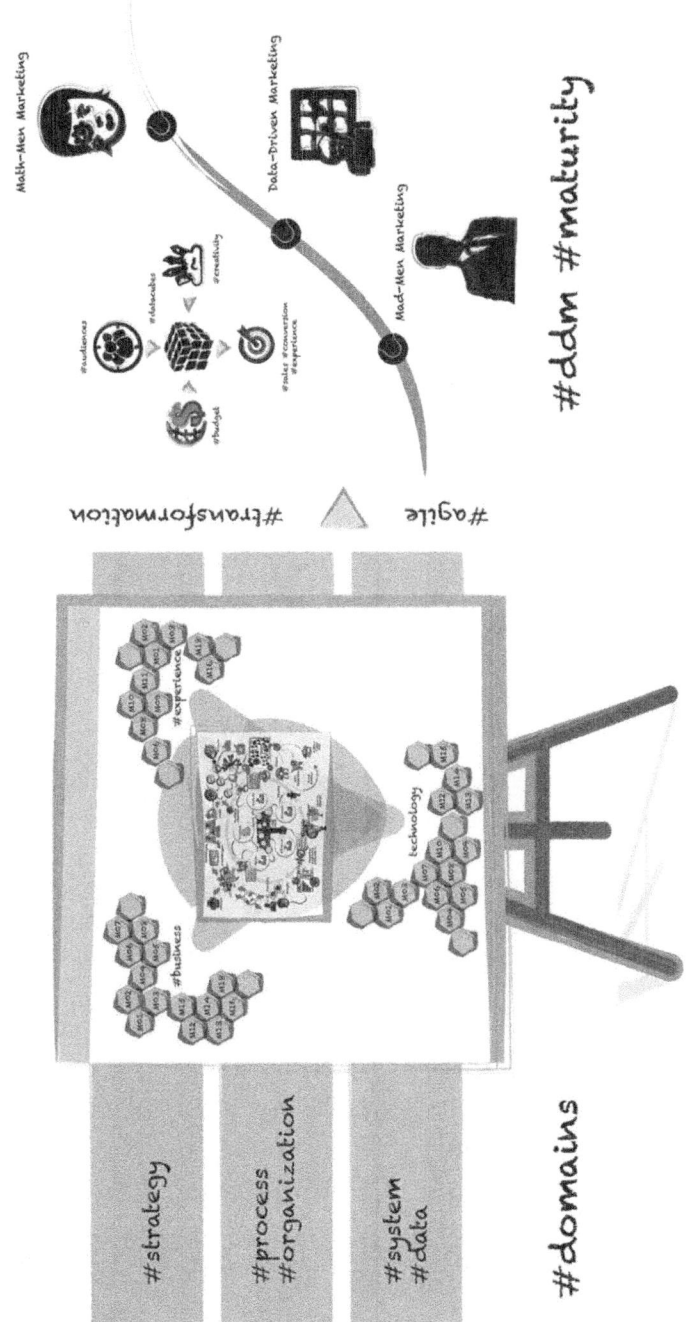

By reaching the champions league and showing you how to transform your marketing department from mad-men towards math-men operating models, I'd like to close this chapter and ultimately, the book. For me, writing down all these thoughts of applying physics to marketing was a real pleasure. I hope you as a reader had some fun with this book.

I hope that some of the ideas will find a way in your new intelligent data-driven way of doing marketing.

Works Cited

Brinker, S., 2020. *Marketing Technology Landscape Supergraphic (2020).* [Online] Available at: https://chiefmartec.com/2020/04/marketing-technology-landscape-2020-martech-5000/

Christensen, C. M., 1997. *The Innovator's Dilemma: When New Technologies Cause Great Firms to Fail.* s.l.: Harvard Business School Press.

Elsässer, M., S. G. H. a. M. W., 1997. Subpicosecond switch-off and switch-on of a semiconductor laser due to transient hot carrier effects. *Applied Physics Letters* 70, p. 853.

Fernandez, J., 2011. *https://www.marketingweek.com/.* [Online] Available at: https://www.marketingweek.com/how-the-old-spice-hunk-took-over-the-world/

Goldratt, E. M., 2004. *The Goal: A Process of Ongoing Improvement.* s.l.: North River Press.

Harari, Y. N., 2014. *Homo Sapiens: a brief history of humankind.* London: Harvill Secker.

Jeffery, M., 2010. *Data-Driven Marketing: The 15 Metrics Everyone in Marketing Should Know.* s.l.:Wiley.

McCrory, D., 2010. *Data Gravitas.* [Online] Available at: https://datagravitas.com/2010/12/07/data-gravity-in-the-clouds/

Österle, H. & Winter, R., 2003. *Business Engineering-Auf dem Weg zum Unternehmen des Informationszeitalters.* Berlin et al: Springer.

Piercy, N. F., 2001. *Market-led strategic change.* Oxford: Butterworth-Heinemann.

Porter, M. E., 1985. *The Competitive Advantage: Creating and Sustaining Superior Performance.* s.l.:NY: Free Press.

Sagovsky, J. C. &. M., 1963. Net Audiences of British Newspapers: A Comparison of the Agostini and Sainsbury Methods. *Journal of Advertising Research,* Issue March, pp. 21–25.

Senge, P. M., 1999. *The Dance of Change: The Challenges of Sustaining Momentum in a Learning Organization.* s.l.:Wiley Periodicals, Inc., A Wiley Company.

Sutherland, J., 2014. *Scrum: The Art of Doing Twice the Work in Half the Time.* New York, NY: Crown Business.

Wikipedia, 2017. *Wikipedia.* [Online] Available at: https://en.wikipedia.org/wiki/Barometer_question.

Wikipedia, 2021. *Wikipedia.* [Online] Available at: https://en.wikipedia.org/wiki/Correlation_does_not_imply_causation.